THE
EMPOWERMENT
OF TEACHERS
OVERCOMING THE CRISIS OF CONFIDENCE

Other books by Gene I. Maeroff

School and College: Partnerships in Education

Don't Blame the Kids: The Trouble with America's Public Schools

The Guide to Suburban Public Schools (with Leonard Buder)

THE
EMPOWERMENT
OF TEACHERS

OVERCOMING THE CRISIS OF CONFIDENCE

GENE I. MAEROFF

TEACHERS
COLLEGE
PRESS

Teachers College, Columbia University
New York and London

To My Teachers

In Elementary School
 Ms. Hurley, who taught me to read
 Ms. Milner, who took me from print to script

In Junior High
 Ms. Dick, who instilled within me my love of American history
 Mr. Tubaugh, who introduced me to journalism

In High School
 Mr. McAfee, who actually made geometry fun
 Ms. Van Sickle, marvelous Ms. Van Sickle, who helped me
  see that writing was to be my life's work

Published by Teachers College Press, 1234 Amsterdam Avenue,
New York, NY 10027

Library of Congress Cataloging-in-Publication Data

Maeroff, Gene I.
  The empowerment of teachers.

  Bibliography: p.
  Includes index.
  1. Teacher morale — United States. 2. Occupational
prestige — United States. I. Title.
LB2840.M28   1988   371.1′023   87-37450

ISBN 0-8077-2908-6

Manufactured in the United States of America

93 92 91 90   3   4   5   6

CONTENTS

FOREWORD

THREE YOUNG SCHOOLTEACHERS, fresh from the first days of class in an urban school, faced an audience of parents and other teachers. One question to them is direct: "You are well-educated and talented people; all of you tried other careers before determining to teach. What brought you to this school, and what would it take to get more young people like you into teaching?"

"Respect," said the teacher in the middle, and both of the others nodded in agreement. "In this school, teachers are respected for their ideas. We are expected to be professionals in our fields." In the school where these three work, teaching is the central mission; teachers are valued professionals, who create an environment of constant learning, for themselves as well as for their students. It is a school known for its excitement and energy.

Gene Maeroff's book is about respect for teachers, and about the excitement and energy it produces. He writes about the importance of improving the status of teachers, the importance of renewing the ideas and information that they take into their classrooms. He writes about the power of such professionalism, and he shows how that power can transform schools. *The Empowerment of Teachers* is a challenging contribution to the national quest for better schools, because it argues that teachers themselves must be leaders of that quest.

Maeroff writes that this book is "not a radical treatise." That may be true, but it is certainly not a usual or an obvious one within the range of studies on the schools. As recently as 1981, in a preface to two volumes of *Daedalus* devoted to portraits of American schools, the editor could write that "the 'unfinished' figures in these portraits are principally the teachers." He lists the many specific questions that are not addressed about the professional lives, the preparation and proficiencies of teachers, despite their importance, even their "absolute centrality" in the schools. That strange lacuna in our learning about schools has changed, but slowly, as interest in the schools has accelerated and widened through the 1980s.

Widespread interest in school reform can virtually be dated from the release in 1983 of *A Nation at Risk*, the report of a blue-ribbon commission appointed by the then U.S. secretary of education, T. H. Bell. Produced by university presidents, education experts, and administrators (one teacher was on the panel), the report commanded immediate and startling attention, flying to the front pages of newspapers all over the country. Whether it released a deep concern within the society about its schools, or created that public concern, the report was timely, unexpectedly so. It set the stage for public attention to the schools, and it claimed attention for many other commissions and studies. The public debate about school reform was on.

Provocative and important as it is, *A Nation at Risk* emphasizes the problems in America's schools rather than detailing causes or possible educational cures. And basically, the teachers are treated as one of the problems. The report's "findings regarding teaching" are all negative. In its list of nine "tools at hand" that should be mobilized for educational reform, teachers are mentioned fleetingly. The report's list of recommendations about teaching centers on getting better people into it. In its section on implementation, the report calls for leadership from ten different groups or sectors of the society to bring about reform. Teachers are not mentioned.

In many of the reports that appeared at this time, the same kind of bare attention to teachers persists. In a 1983 Twentieth Century Fund report, for instance, recommendations for change are based on an assumption of an absolute "deterioration" in the "quality of teaching." Later reports begin to provide some corrective to this.

For instance, in *Horace's Compromise*, Theodore R. Sizer's examination of "The Dilemma of the American High School," teachers are more sympathetically viewed. Caught between unyielding demands— large classes and tight schedules on the one hand, his own high ideals and his love of his subject on the other—Sizer's representative teacher, although he is the "key" to reform, is rendered immobile. Dulled by the demands on him, he reflects the immobility of the system that contains him. It follows, in Sizer's view and that of other critics, that the solution must be a complete change in the system: the creation of "effective schools," less centralized schools, to replace those that have paralyzed learning. Sizer proposes administrative solutions by which teachers will be freed, less compromised. Other reformers similarly argue for better schools management, for the primacy of principals in school reform, for the necessity of firmer local control of the schools. The Holmes Group of leading teacher educators, which is also supportive of teachers, offers another kind of administrative solution when it argues for changes in the certification of teachers as the basis for reform. In these reports, teachers are viewed, quite persuasively, as prisoners who can be set free by better management. Teacher professionalism and participation are clear goals of reform in these studies, but they tend to portray teachers, in their solutions as in their analyses, as essentially passive recipients of reform initiatives.

More recent reports and studies portray teachers as more active protagonists in the drama of school reform. In its scenario for schools in the twenty-first century, for instance, the 1986 report on teaching of the Carnegie Forum on Education and the Economy envisions schools in which teachers help decide what should be taught and how. The Metropolitan Life survey of *The American Teacher 1986* focuses on the participation of teachers in school management. In a study called "The Teacher: Ally in Educational Reform," the Work in America Institute envisions schools with dramatically more autonomous teachers, who are specifically charged with the responsibility of making education in their schools better.

It is to this vision of teachers as active participants in school reform that Gene Maeroff speaks. He offers arguments for the increased autonomy of teachers, for the creative power of teachers to make instructional change; he offers examples from the field—from the classrooms, the teachers' rooms, the cafeterias and playgrounds where teachers exercise their commitment and their hopes for reform. It is Maeroff's thesis that changing teachers' lives will change the schools.

There is, I think we must agree, little evidence of a scientific kind for this thesis. There is no great body of data that shows the effect on particular schools or students of trusting teachers more, or of improving their status as professionals in their disciplines. There are no before-and-after statistics, no improved scores, to quantify the results of greater teacher involvement in curriculum. The arguments are largely anecdotal or—to be more precise—they derive from accumulated observations. Maeroff offers the collected evidence of the good journalist. He has talked with teachers in the field and with the administrators, officials, and concerned citizens around them. He has watched teachers renew their understanding in workshops and courses; he has seen them share ideas and experiences in the schools; he has witnessed their work to improve curriculum and to add resources to their classrooms. His book is a testament to dedicated teachers and to the educational changes that can result if that dedication is trusted.

As Maeroff makes clear throughout his text, a number of experiments and projects have focused on teachers in recent years. Fostered by individual educators, by universities, or directly by school systems, funded by private foundations, local businesses, and by school boards or unions, a number of programs center on teachers, and Maeroff describes many of them. The program mounted by the Rockefeller Foundation is in no way nobler than the others, but it does provide an illustration of the opportunities and problems such an approach provides. For that purpose, it has been useful to the author.

The Foundation's program is called CHART (Collaboratives for Humanities and Arts Teaching). It is a network of quite distinct, locally based partnerships in nine school systems across the country, which are intended to provide training, incentives, and other professional opportunities for humanities teachers. For the Foundation, CHART has also illustrated the need for flexibility in establishing expectations, and even goals, within a program. The Foundation's expectations and goals have evolved over the four years that have gone into the creation of the schools network.

Originally, with the help of a panel of experts in education, we set several goals for our work in the schools. The primary purpose would be to provide resources for the disciplines of the humanities in the school improvement movement to parallel the efforts in science, math, and vocational areas that were certain to get attention. This has been an easier task than we had predicted. The importance of reading and writing, of the renewed significance of understanding American history and the cultures and languages of other countries, has been well comprehended by the schools and their supporters. The National Endowment for the Humanities, with redesigned programs for humanities education first announced in 1982, has certainly been an instrumental force in this salutary development.

A second purpose, one we have shared with a great many other agencies, has been the building of collaborations, partnerships of public and private supporters, for the schools. Here again, along with many other agencies, the Foundation has found partnerships with other sectors easier to build and more important for change than had been predicted. Without enlightened superintendents and principals, school reform would simply not be possible. We found many such administrators. Without flexible and forward-looking union leaders, little could be achieved. We found that leadership, too. And without the contributions of corporate, cultural, and higher education leaders, much less would be possible; we have found these sectors ready to support public education. If, as Maeroff reminds us, there is much recalcitrance and misunderstanding about teachers in these sectors, there is also much openness and readiness for shared action.

The third purpose we named for ourselves turned out to be the most important; that is, the focus on teachers as the key agents in school reform. This is the subject of Maeroff's study, and it is also the subject, in my view, of greatest discovery and reward in today's reform activity. Ambitious plans for cross-sector partnership, for systemwide programming, for curricular innovations, or for administrative change can be unsuccessful, but work with the teachers seldom fails. When teachers set out to improve their own learning and their contributions to schooling, it is thrilling to see the depths of their concern for their disciplines and their students, the energy they are willing to put into their work, the degree to which they can renew themselves and their classrooms, and their readiness to rededicate themselves.

For our discovery of the importance of this part of our own program, we are much indebted to Gene Maeroff. During 1986, he worked as a consultant on our education projects and began to identify for us the concrete accomplishments of the teachers in the projects and their potential for making change in their schools. When Maeroff decided that there was a book about teacher enpowerment that needed to be written, and that would draw on examples in our program and in others, he ceased to consult for the Foundation. We were proud to make a grant to him to work as an independent author. We have waited eagerly to read what he would say about teachers, about the process of empowerment, and about the role of school systems and sponsors and communities in improving the status of teachers.

What he offers in *The Empowerment of Teachers* is a compelling portrait of teachers, determined and burdened, underacknowledged but eager, cynical yet hopeful, ready to recommit themselves to the schools and to the students. Admiring America's teachers becomes easy as Maeroff shows them to us. Encouraging them, acknowledging their professional importance, and helping them utilize their strengths must follow.

Other readers will surely feel indebted, as we do, to Gene Maeroff's wise, well-informed commitment to public education, his persistent regard for the importance of every individual teacher, and his keen sensitivity to professionalism in teaching and in journalism.

ALBERTA ARTHURS
Director for Arts and Humanities
The Rockefeller Foundation

PREFACE

THE TEACHER is the basis of schooling. This observation is so self-evident that it seems not worth making. Yet, many of the reforms proposed for elementary and secondary education seem not to take note of the primacy of the teacher. It is as if teachers were part of the inanimate classroom — like the books, the desks, the computers, and the chalkboards. Those who seek to impose rigid day-by-day instructional objectives on the schools give the impression that teachers are little more than talking textbooks on which dials can be turned to make them go through their presentations more quickly or more slowly, as needed.

But the input of teachers must give shape to the forming of education; it cannot be left to others to make all the important decisions. Flesh and blood require more nurturing than do plastic and steel. Unless teachers are treated with humaneness and dignity, the education of children cannot fulfill its potential. In part, taking greater regard of teachers and what they have to say means enhancing their role. Knowledgeable teachers who act as professionals can improve the education of their students. This is the reason why teachers should be empowered.

This book is not a radical treatise. Critics may say it does not go far enough. But if the lessons gleaned from the projects, as reflected on these pages, are carried to their conclusion, the resulting change in the position of teachers would set the stage for almost any degree of empowerment desired. In other words, once teachers are raised in status, made more competent at their craft, and given entrée to the decision-making process, the rest will follow.

Such a book as this would have been inappropriate just a few years ago. The collective bargaining movement was not sufficiently mature to allow teachers to proceed to the negotiating table in a spirit of collaboration. The reform movement had not underscored the need for changing the old order in the schools. Teachers were still too militant and principals were still too defensive in trying to uphold an employer–employee relationship that was more concerned with determining who was the subordinate and who was in charge.

Change is in the air today. *A Nation at Risk* opened a door to reform that had long been jammed shut. The report of the Holmes Group showed that there were leading teacher educators who believed that the time was right to embark on a fresh road for preparing teachers who would expect no less than other professionals to share power in the workplace. The report of the Carnegie Forum's Task Force provided — if not a blueprint — at least a starting point for discussions about how to professionalize teaching.

I am indebted to the Rockefeller Foundation for making it possible for me to examine its Secondary Schools Humanities Program, now known as CHART— Collaboratives for Humanities and Arts Teaching. I am grateful for the encouragement to search for the elements of empowerment that the program opened to teachers. My study was unfettered, and Richard Lyman, president of the Rockefeller Foundation, urged me to identify as many of the foibles of the program as possible. My problem was that in more than two decades as an education writer I had seldom come across a project in which the teachers were more enthusiastic in their praise.

This does not mean that the program was perfect or even that it will outlast the Foundation's involvement — though I suspect it will. But it is clear that the program struck a responsive chord among teachers, satisfying unmet needs and opening their eyes to professional deprivations with which they had been conditioned to live. The teachers also discovered that principals and other administrators can, in the right circumstances, be allies and not enemies. Full empowerment, however, is still a long way off, and I do not want to sound so enthusiastic that it appears that I do not recognize the length of the road yet to be traveled. The distance is far, but as the proverb says, the longest journey starts with the first step.

I interviewed so many people in writing this book and consulted with so many experts that I will not risk trying to name them all. But I do want to recognize the project directors for CHART who helped me so much during my visits to their cities: Ellyn Berk in New York, Peggy Funkhouser in Los Angeles, Jim Grob in Seattle, Judith Hodgson in Philadelphia, Molly LaBerge in Saint Paul, Paul LeMahieu in Pittsburgh, Dennis Lubeck in St. Louis, and John Paskus in Atlanta. Also, I want to take special note of the aid provided to me during visits to the sites of the Ford Foundation's Urban Mathematics Collaborative Project by Paula Anderson in Cleveland, Gladys Thacher in San Francisco, and

Constance Barkley in New Orleans. Similarly, I owe thanks to Marv Jaffe in connection with my visit to Westport, Connecticut, Ellen Dempsey in New York for my research into Impact II, Barbara Nelson at the Ford Foundation, and Karin Egan at the Carnegie Corporation. As always, I am grateful for the wonderful library at Teachers College, Columbia University.

Finally, my deepest appreciation goes to my colleagues at the Rockefeller Foundation who were so very much a part of this enterprise. In the first place, CHART would not exist if Alberta Arthurs and Steven Lavine had not created it. So without them there would not have been a program about which to write. But so far as my personal involvement is concerned, I was helped immeasurably by their cooperation, confidence, and candor. I thank them for their generosity of spirit and wish I could be blessed always with such colleagues in my endeavors as an education writer.

THE
EMPOWERMENT
OF TEACHERS
OVERCOMING THE CRISIS OF CONFIDENCE

1 ▶▶

GETTING STARTED

LIZ WOODS, a veteran English teacher in Philadelphia, thought that the need for raising the morale and status of big city schoolteachers was profound. "There is no way I can say it strongly enough," Woods remarked. "In the typical school you are isolated, cut off from everyone. The rest of the culture outside the school doesn't give a damn about you or about the kids you are trying to teach. The school system itself almost regards you in that way. You are in the place where the bells are ringing, but the people who are calling the signals for the schools are in places where they can't even hear the bells."

This impotence, this absence of power felt by Woods and other teachers, especially those in urban school systems, is what often causes pessimism over the possibility of improvement. They find themselves assigned one of the most difficult tasks a society can give, and yet they do not feel they have the authority to do what is expected of them or the recognition that they think the job ought to carry. At a time that a powerful school reform movement is sweeping across America not enough is being done to address the needs of teachers, the group upon whom change is most dependent.

Despite the centrality of the teacher's role in determining what happens in schools, many of the reports on school reform, beginning with *A Nation at Risk* (1983), emphasized altering the outward structure—a longer school day, a longer school year, more of this subject, more of that subject. Such changes hold promise and can be important, but in the end it is the teacher who is going to make the most difference. If elementary and secondary education in America improves, it will be, more than anything else, because of the part teachers play. Nonetheless, the teacher's role is often ignored in the recommendations for improving schools.

Thus, it was gratifying, at last, to see two national reports on school improvement in 1986 that paid particular attention to teachers. The reports by the Carnegie Forum's Task Force on Teaching as a Profession and by the Education Commission of the States were by no means the first or the only ones to feature teachers, but their single-mindedness in focusing on teachers was a special contribution to the reform movement. One of the most intriguing features of their proposals was the idea that teachers must have more power, more authority for what happens in the school.

"Giving teachers a greater voice in the decisions that affect the school will make teaching more attractive to good teachers who are already in our schools as well as people considering teaching as a career," the Carnegie Forum stated (p. 57). It was a view echoed by the Education Commission of the States: "Nobody reports to the teacher. The teacher reports to everyone else. Other people decide almost everything—how the day is organized, how students are assigned, what the curriculum will be, what is the day-to-day scope and sequence of instruction, how discipline is meted out. The schools operate in an incredibly bureaucratic culture, at the bottom of which we find the teacher. That makes schools very unattractive to many people with real intellectual skills and the desire for some control over themselves and their environment."

Teachers are expected to act as professionals, but they are told to take on tasks that are assuredly nonprofessional and decidedly demeaning. "Two years ago, I spent the beginning of every school day watching people park their cars, making sure students didn't park in the teachers' spaces," said Lloyd A. Johnson, the chairman of the mathematics department at a high school in a small town in Connecticut. "The year before that, I stood in the courtyard watching students smoke. For another 45-minute period, I watched students study and signed corridor passes to exciting places like the lavatory and the library."

More than altruism is involved in trying to alter the circumstances of teaching. If the job is so undesirable that not enough qualified people want it, then there may be an awful lot of kids without anyone to teach their classes in the 1990s. The reality is that teacher shortages are already developing and are expected to grow worse in the next decade, when the higher birthrate of the 1980s will push enrollments back up, though there are serious differences over how critical the shortages will be. The Western Interstate Commission on Higher Education, pinpointing the problem in just one region of the country, predicts a severe shortage of teachers in the 1990s in Alaska, Nevada, and Wyoming and more moderate shortages in most other western states.

There is a paradox in discussions of teachers and power. On the one hand, teachers ostensibly have more freedom in their work than do those in many occupations. When the classroom door closes, the teacher typically has enormous latitude in deciding how to teach a lesson. Teachers spend most of their working time out of sight of any supervisor. Granted that students and the parents of students look over the shoulders of teachers, but they do so no less than patients and clients who keep their eyes on physicians and lawyers. Journalists have a reading public and businesspeople have customers. So the fact is that aside from infrequent observation by a principal or some other administrator the teacher is essentially on his or her own. It is true there are lesson plans to file and reams of forms to fill out, but, despite the carping by teachers, accountability by paperwork is not unique to their craft.

What is it then that makes the situation different for teachers? For one thing, teaching, more than many other occupations, is practiced in isolation, an isolation that is at times crushing in its separateness. Is power conferred on someone simply by leaving him or her alone? Collegiality is nonexistent for many teachers, unless hurried lunches over plastic trays in unkempt lunchrooms are viewed as exercises in colleagueship, rather than the complaint sessions they are more likely to be. Knowledge is the currency in which a teacher deals, and yet the teacher's own knowledge is allowed to become stale and devalued, as though ideas were not the lifeblood of the occupation. The circumstances of teaching, exacerbated by the relatively meager salaries, add up to a status so low that often teachers do not respect themselves or each other.

"Perceptive researchers have told us for years that teachers are treated as if they have no expertise worth having," the Carnegie Forum said (p. 39). "An endless array of policies succeed in constraining the exercise of the teacher's independent judgment on almost every matter of moment. There may be some who believe that all this is fully justified by what they perceive as teachers of inadequate ability. But the plain fact is that the many good teachers we have are being driven out of teaching by these conditions, and it will be impossible to attract many new people of real ability to teaching until conditions are radically altered."

Proposals are flowing forth for converting teaching into the profession it is often called but that it really is not. Eventually there are likely to be changes in the way that those headed into teaching are educated, certified, and licensed. Salaries are even rising; the abysmal $14,500 paid to starting teachers in New York City, the nation's largest school district, was raised to $20,000 over a period of just two years and is to reach $25,000 in 1990. There also may be some fundamental changes in the job assignments of teachers, with those of greater demonstrated ability getting increased responsibility and higher pay than others.

Giving teachers greater power is a major way to make them more professional and to improve their performance. Professionals usually have a sense of authority about what they do and are recognized as experts in their fields. They feel good about themselves and are respected by others. The empowerment of teachers has to do with their individual deportment, not their ability to boss others. The kind of power discussed in this book is not of the strutting, order-issuing variety. It is the power to exercise one's craft with confidence and to help shape the way that the job is to be done. This is the teacher empowerment with which this book deals. The "confidence" to which this book refers is the confidence teachers have in themselves and the confidence others have in teachers.

Teams organized to conduct interactive research on schooling found that what enabled some teachers to maintain positive attitudes about their jobs were the freedom to be creative and innovative, the capacity to influence students, opportunities for feedback, recognition and support, and the chance to share with peers (Lieberman, 1986). Such is the stuff of which empowerment is made.

ROCKEFELLER'S HUMANITIES PROGRAM (CHART)

There is surely no single way to empower teachers and to improve the circumstances of their employment. But some insight into what is needed and what is possible can be gleaned by careful examination of attempts to achieve these goals. One such effort was the Rockefeller Foundation's program to strengthen arts and humanities education in the secondary schools, CHART. It began in 1983 in Philadelphia and then expanded with grants for projects in Atlanta, Los Angeles, New York City, Pittsburgh, St. Louis, Saint Paul, Seattle, and a group of rural school districts in South Carolina. (For a description of the programs, see chapter 7.) Mostly big cities were selected as the stages on which to carry out this performance because the problems of urban education are so severe and the teachers who work in such settings have the greatest need for uplifting.

The outward aim of the program was to promote improvement in the teaching of arts and humanities in the schools. This concern was prompted by the findings in 1980 of the blue-ribbon commission, formed by the Rockefeller Foundation, that studied "The Humanities in American Life." A key recommendation of the panel was that the schools were the place to begin building a life-long appreciation of the humanities. Acting on this idea, the Foundation encouraged the development of ventures to enable teachers of the arts and humanities to collaborate with cultural institutions, businesses, and colleges. This effort took on special significance at a time when the arts and humanities in schools were being eclipsed by technology, which some external critics of education said was far more crucial to the future lives of students.

On its surface, then, the Humanities Program was just one more exercise in strengthening teaching in a specific portion of the curriculum, in this case the arts and humanities. On a deeper level, though, there was an agenda not immediately apparent except to the extent that CHART was described by Rockefeller as an effort to improve the status and training of teachers. At its core, the endeavor sought to empower teachers. Teaching in the arts and humanities was to be the vehicle for that empowerment. It was not so much a clandestine goal as it was a subtle one.

By raising their morale, deepening their intellectual background, and giving them access to decision making, the designers of the program hoped that teachers would gain the confidence and ability to leave the stultifying safety of their nests and stretch their fledgling wings. So the subject of this book about teacher empowerment is a program that set out to help teachers learn how to be better teachers. Some of them worked on their writing; others conferred with colleagues to develop interdisciplinary units. Some social studies teachers learned about parts of the world that had seldom been part of the lessons they taught, while other teachers deepened their knowledge of subjects that they had been teaching for years. The context in which this was done — bringing together the resources of higher education, business, and cultural institutions — and the way the teachers were treated during this program were crucial. The fact that teams of teachers from the same school were involved and that the program ran through the summer and the school year helped make it different. The aim of this book is to identify how these various elements came together in ways that advanced teacher empowerment.

There are, of course, many possible ways to pursue these objectives, and CHART was certainly not the only way to go about it. But in viewing teacher empowerment primarily through the prism of this one national endeavor there are lessons for teachers everywhere. While this book focuses mostly on the Rockefeller project, some of the same elements have been part of programs operated by the Ford Foundation, the Carnegie Corporation, and other foundations, as well as by such federal agencies as the National Endowment for the Humanities and the National Science Foundation.

In fact, both the teacher enhancement program of the National Science Foundation and the elementary and secondary schools program operated by the education division of the National Endowment for the Humanities (NEH) are far larger than the series of secondary schools humanities programs run by the Rockefeller Foundation. But the purpose here is not to identify which is biggest or even best, nor to say that Rockefeller alone was responsible for what occurred through CHART. Though Rockefeller provided the fiscal spark that ignited the program, the effort was sustained by many local funders and their contributions eventually were more than twice as great as Rockefeller's. The point is not to find out who spent the most money, but rather to examine in depth one particular program that combined elements in a special way, providing fresh understanding of what is needed to transform the inservice education of teachers into an experience in empowerment.

The Elements of Empowerment

Various states and individual colleges and school systems also have sponsored programs for teachers that helped them stride toward empowerment. References are made to these programs, too, but they are mentioned less often so that the book can be unified by its concentration on one program. Rather than try to provide a compendium of every such effort, this book focuses mostly on the one program and examines the implications for teacher empowerment. Empowerment, as viewed in this book, is a term somewhat synonymous with professionalization. It does not necessarily mean being in charge, though that is possible; more than anything else it means working in an environment in which a teacher acts as a professional and is treated as a professional. The inevitable result is empowerment. Toward that end, there are three guiding principles that appear and reappear in these pages.

- Boosting status is fundamental to the process because, simply put, those who have lost the will are not likely to find the way. Teachers themselves make it abundantly clear that the ability to look at themselves and their colleagues through new eyes has liberated them from the self-imposed shackles of low esteem.
- Making teachers more knowledgeable is an obvious step in enhancing their power. Francis Bacon said it long ago, and it has never been said better: "Knowledge is power." Part of the reason why teachers have not exerted more authority is because they are not sufficiently well informed to do so. A teacher not versed in

history must assuredly depend on others to supply a curriculum for a history course. A teacher intimidated by mathematics is not likely to be able to critique a textbook. Teachers shaky in their academic and pedagogical backgrounds must repeatedly defer to the judgments of supervisors, who are given the time to be the supposed experts.

- Finally, allowing teachers access to the lofty towers of power means building psychological ladders they may climb to escape their isolation and gain the overview that few of them usually attain. It also means connecting teachers with each other and with principals, building a kind of collegiality that has been all too unusual in elementary and secondary schools.

The links to power are strengthened when teachers can galvanize them with ties to colleagues in higher education and in the corporate world. Giving teachers a taste of the sort of authority that others have over their own professions can encourage teachers in their pursuit. This is important because teachers judge the potential for their empowerment mostly by what they have known in schools, a view that until now has been skewed. "Traditionally, power in public education flows down from school board to superintendent to principal. The teacher's only power is at the bargaining table and in the classroom — but only over the children and under rules imposed from above" (Hechinger, 1986).

Empowerment can garb itself in many guises. Surely, teachers who have absolute and final authority in running a school are powerful to the extreme. There are not many such schools, but there are a few. Such a prominent role, while one possible model, is probably not necessary, though, for teachers to feel stronger and more confident and to do a better job with their students. Thus, the premise here is not that empowerment means running the show. In fact, many teachers say they do not want responsibility for all the decisions in their schools. What they desire is that their voices be heard and respected. They want their needs and opinions reflected in the policies of the school and the district. Empowerment of teachers need not mean that principals cease being in charge, but it should mean much more consultation and collaborative deliberation.

Implementing the Elements

Involvement alone is not enough; it leaves too much room for tokenism. Genuine influence is needed. For our purposes, teachers who have influence can affect outcomes. Influence is crucial to empowerment. In his model of power, Muth (1984) labeled influence a subtype of power, that is, the ability—without legitimation or recourse to force—to affect the behavior of others. He wrote that it came from using persuasion to convince others that the desired behavior will be beneficial to them. Even without being in charge, teachers who have status, knowledge, and access can wield this kind of influence.

So long as teachers are diminished by their status they are bound to feel weak. So long as teachers do not have a firm grasp of the subjects they are asked to teach they are apt to feel inadequate. So long as they have no connection to the decision-making process they are going to regard themselves as outsiders. John Goodlad (1984) concluded, after interviewing 1,350 teachers for his exhaustive study *A Place Called School*: "If teachers are potentially powerfully influential in the education of children and youth in school but the circumstances of teaching inhibit their functioning, then we need to modify these circumstances so as to maximize teachers' potential. The directions of school improvement become reasonably clear: diagnose and seek to remedy the impending conditions; improve teachers' knowledge and skills."

All of this said, the problem remains one of activating the mechanisms that will lead to greater status, knowledge, and access so that teachers may edge closer to empowerment. Pieces of the combination have been offered through many programs over the years. The "teacher of the year" has been recognized in various ways by local school districts, states, and even at the national level. Achieving such distinction has undoubtedly been a boon to the winners. Teachers have been selected for the privilege of studying in National Science Foundation institutes and similar programs that have increased their knowledge of subject matter and made them more powerful in exercising their craft. Teachers have served on committees to design curriculum and select textbooks and they have even had a hand in running schools where faculty members share in governance.

But implementing such changes widely and making them last is not easy within the school bureaucracy. Layer upon layer of authority, like coats of paint on a piece of old furniture, have in most school districts created an impenetrably thick veneer. Doing anything for teachers that will empower them becomes cumbersome within the average school system, which transforms itself slowly and tends to perpetuate the status quo. There is, for instance, the whole issue of a teacher's time. It is fine to talk of letting teachers assume more authority over school-wide matters, but how is that to happen when teachers barely have free moments during the day to go to the toilet and when they run out of time at night for marking papers? Are schools prepared to hire more personnel so that teachers will be released from some of the commitments that are now basic to the job? Can school systems be expected to take steps in this direction without being forced to do so?

THE OUTSIDE AGENCY

Thus, rather than trying to alter the situation from within, change might be promoted more effectively from the outside. The Rockefeller Foundation, for example, set out to implement its program by work-ing — in most cases — through outside agencies with links to the schools, instead of dealing directly or solely with school systems. The outside organization, or so-called local education fund, is usually beyond the day-to-day control of the school system, giving it independence and flexibility. It has the ability to work around bureaucratic obstacles. Exemplifying this exogenous arrangement are such agencies as the Los Angeles Educational Partnership and the Philadelphia Alliance for Teaching Humanities in the Schools. There are now dozens of these entities across the country, the midwife to many of them having been the Public Education Fund, a group supported by the Ford Foundation in the mid-1980s for the specific purpose of helping form local agencies.

"One of the basic assumptions of the local education fund strategy is that in order to carry out their mission of support for the public schools such funds must be a neutral, third party agency," stated the evaluation report of the Public Education Fund (1986). Such organiza-tions, acting as brokers and intermediaries, try to draw on the resources of the community — business, higher education, and cultural institu-tions — to assist the public schools. The idea is that there are many resources available in any big city that could help improve public educa-tion if the right matches could be effected.

Typical of this role was what the San Francisco Education Fund did when it found out that a small private foundation wanted to give $90,000 to the public school system but sought to do so in a way that would maximize the impact of the grant. It was determined that ele-mentary school libraries would be ideal beneficiaries because cutbacks had caused them to lose both librarians and budgets for book acquisi-tion. The donor, though, was concerned that money might be spent for books that would sit on the shelves. So, with the San Francisco Educa-tion Fund playing a key role, a program was devised that would be limited to about 10 elementary schools to focus the impact, and ar-rangements were made to consult the teachers in those schools about the books to be purchased.

The outside organization may have more credibility with teachers than the school system has. "Teachers are much more willing to participate in a program because it is coming from Compas and not imposed on them by the school system," said Carole Martignacco, former director of the Dialogue program that Compas sponsored in Saint Paul in connection with CHART to help teachers improve their writing ability and, in turn, the writing of their students. "They feel that if it is imposed by the district their performance will be monitored and it will affect their employment. The psychological differences have a lot to do with the success of the program."

Even administrators echo this view, tacitly acknowledging, in effect, that the school system bureaucracy of which they are part is not always the best mechanism for action. "The principals see the Los Angeles Educational Partnership as efficient and well organized, as an organization that understands the needs of the educational community," said Daniel M. Isaacs, an assistant superintendent in Los Angeles. And Catherine C. Hatala, director of reading, English, and language arts for the public schools in Philadelphia, thought that in the eyes of teachers the school system could not bring the same prestige to a program — or as readily capture the confidence of teachers — as an outside agency could, especially an agency that carries the imprimatur of foundations that have provided it with funds.

Some of the activities in which these outside organizations have gotten involved, aside from anything having to do with the content of CHART, are the following:

Fund-raising. Often, they act as development arms of the school systems, receiving donations that can then be dispersed and spent in behalf of the public schools. The contributions come from foundations, corporations, and private donors.

Advice giving. Sharing knowledge and expertise can sometimes be as important as giving money. What the organizations can do is facilitate contacts so that people, principally professors and business executives, can consult with schoolteachers and administrators on many problems and issues.

Public relations. Most big city school systems, unfortunately, have poor reputations. The outside organizations may mount campaigns, sometimes using advertising, to build the image of public education. They also may urge people who are sending their children to private and parochial schools to consider enrolling them in the public schools. Besides improving the reputation of the school system, these activities can boost the morale of students and teachers in the system, making them feel better about the enterprise of which they are part.

Sponsoring educational programs. Very often the outside organization itself uses money from grants and donations to work with teachers and administrators. It gets involved in such activities, for example, as the teaching of writing across the curriculum in Philadelphia or global education in New York.

Working directly with teachers and/or administrators. This approach is related to the previous one in that it is usually tied to a program sponsored by the organization. There might be speakers brought in for seminars during the school year or dinners for teachers and principals with business executives. There might be institutes for principals or interdisciplinary meetings to bring together high school and college teachers of the same subject.

Getting Leverage from the Outside

The last two functions described were the basis for the involvement of the outside agencies in Rockefeller's Collaboratives for Humanities and Arts Teaching. What is crucial about the outside organization and why it can act in behalf of teachers in ways that the school system usually finds more difficult is that it operates in a never-never land where one foot is inside the school system and the other outside. The organization is not under the aegis of school authorities, keeping it purer in the eyes of teachers.

School systems, of course, are not evil entities, but often the practical reality is that they do not have the ability to be advocates for teachers in the way that someone working from an outside base does. Laurence Devine, a teacher in Philadelphia, said this ability to be flexible while working from the outside was an attribute he appreciated in the outside agency in his city, the Philadelphia Alliance for Teaching Humanities in the Schools (PATHS). "With PATHS you generate ideas and if they like them they fund them," he said. "In the school system that just doesn't happen because there is too much bureaucracy and too little extra money. PATHS provides wonderful opportunities to do things you can't normally do in the confines of a big city system."

For its part, the Ford Foundation, like Rockefeller, chose to work through outside agencies in setting up the Urban Mathematics Collaborative Project, an effort with secondary school mathematics teachers similar to what Rockefeller was attempting to do with teachers of the humanities. In each of the 11 cities in the Ford project an agency external to the public school system was selected as the sponsor and given a grant to carry out the project. Ford officials said they sought a kind of flexibility that they did not think could be found in the bureaucracy of the school system. Ford wanted the sponsoring agency to take chances in behalf of teachers and to be willing to run the risk of failure. This is not the orientation of school systems, which are more oriented — as perhaps they should be — to displaying success.

Also, without independence, there is the risk of what happened in one city where CHART was headed by a director appointed by and reporting to an assistant superintendent instead of to an outside organization. At one point, the assistant superintendent seriously jeopardized the program by reassigning the director to another job; it took considerable discussion between the Rockefeller Foundation and school authorities to get the reassignment rescinded. This is not to say that a program designed to produce change cannot be run from within the school system.

But compared with any school district's total budget, the amount that an outside organization puts into the schools is miniscule — a few million dollars in a budget of hundreds of millions. If this small amount were dropped into the general coffers of the school system, the effect would be largely negligible. Like a bucket of sand emptied onto a beach, it would be indistinguishable — just a few more dollars to do what was already being done. Thus, the money from the outside organization, effectively, is not commingled and the outside organization keeps control over how it is spent, maximizing the impact. The organization may in some projects ask the school system, by way of showing commitment, to provide matching funds from its operating budget to support a project.

In most cases, the outside organization has a board of directors drawn from both the community and the school system. The chairman often is an influential business executive and generally plays a role far beyond that of a mere figurehead. Because of the clout of the board, the organization usually has direct access to the school superintendent when needed.

The purpose here is not to say that CHART brought outside organizations into existence or that outside organizations were formed simply to implement CHART. The support of the Ford Foundation through the Public Education Fund was much more significant in this regard. Such ventures as the Los Angeles Educational Partnership preceded the creation of CHART and were a paradigm for other cities, independent of the launching of the Rockefeller Foundation program. But CHART did provide an additional project for some of these organizations and, in at least one place (Philadelphia) was the program that figured in the initial operations of the outside organization.

When Rockefeller launched CHART what it sought above all else was strong leadership for the boards of the outside organizations that were given the grants to mount the program in the various cities. "I am fundamentally interested in pressing systems toward reform," said Alberta B. Arthurs, director of the Arts and Humanities Program of the Rockefeller Foundation. "You can do that best if you have leadership that will get attention. For example, it is impossible to ignore PATHS in Philadelphia." The visible presence that could not be overlooked in Philadelphia was Ralph S. Saul, former chairman of the CIGNA Corporation and one of the city's leading movers and shakers. He was the founding chairman of the Committee to Support Philadelphia Public Schools. The business organization dipped its toe into the educational waters by setting up the Philadelphia Alliance for Teaching Humanities in the Schools to operate the program that Rockefeller was helping to fund, which has become one of many activities of the Committee. "I felt it was an important piece of work and the timing for it was just right," Saul said. "Business realized it had an important stake in the city's youth and in getting public education to become responsible for producing working citizens."

This initiative by business fortuitously coincided with the early days of Constance Clayton's school superintendency in Philadelphia. Clayton was receptive to fresh ideas and encouraged businesspeople who were wondering what they could do for a school system that had become tarnished in the eyes of many members of the community. In Clayton, they found a leader ready to advance in new directions, one who could flesh out plans in ways that held promise.

What does all this have to do with teachers? Namely, that if the circumstances of teaching are to change and if teachers are to be empowered in ways that improve their work, great care has to go into the mechanisms designed to bring this about. It ought to be clear by now that just giving more money to school systems to spend in the manner in which they have always spent it may not produce much change. Leverage from the outside helps and if CHART had no other value it at least demonstrated this much. "From the very beginning," Arthurs said, "the aim of our program was to work with the power structure of the community. The basic idea was to enhance the teaching profession — to give more attention, authority, and status to what teachers do."

Just how elusive this goal can be, even when pursued through the intervention of an outside organization, can be seen in a tour of the pitfalls that befell CHART at various times in cities across the country. It was viewed as crucial, for example, that teachers participate in the program by choice, not by compulsion. Too many programs in the schools have failed because teachers were ordered to carry them out. Their lack of commitment and absence of enthusiasm gave the teachers no sense of ownership, and they did not care about the programs or feel a vested interest in them. Therefore, school authorities were generally urged to keep participation in CHART voluntary.

Pitfalls in Saint Paul

What this meant in the implementation of CHART in just one school district, Saint Paul, is illustrative of the problem. For school officials working with Compas, the charge to find committed volunteers was first of all mitigated by the school district's need to select schools that would represent the geographic and ethnic composition of the district. Beyond that, officials say they truly tried to avoid any appearance of imposing the program where it was not desired.

"We wanted schools with teachers who would be supportive of the program, where we would not get stonewalled," said Carole Snyder, assistant director of curriculum and instruction for the Saint Paul public schools. "We looked at requests from principals. There were more requests than we could handle. We selected 10 schools for the first year. There was one school we considered, debated about and finally decided not to include. I couldn't predict whether the staff would be supportive. I didn't want to put the program there unless they would be receptive. We didn't want to put the program anyplace where the teachers would think it was a case of our telling them what to do. We wanted them to feel the ownership. The most effective inservice is that in which teachers are involved in the planning and where they think it meets their needs."

That was Snyder's view, formed in obvious good faith, from the vantage of the administrative level. It coincided with the view of other administrators. "For two years we had been working on teaching writing as a process with the goal of improving the writing skills of kids," said Al Saunders, an elementary school principal in Saint Paul. "I saw this program as tying in with that so I applied to have our school join the program. I think we were selected because of our school's commitment to writing. Until then, though, we hadn't done anything to teach teachers to write."

Saunders said he asked for 10 volunteers and got 14. He selected 10 by eliminating those who were closest to retirement. "I wanted the greatest long-term effect for the school," Saunders said. "The perception that the teachers have of my support for the project is crucial. I showed up at three of the four training sessions. After all, more than 50 percent of a principal's job is just showing up one place or another to lend credibility. We're very excited about the Writer in Residence coming to our school. The year will culminate with a Writers Fair in which every student in the school will have writing on display and parents will be invited to come and see the work."

Yet, in spite of Snyder's diligence in seeking schools with a commitment and in spite of the zeal of principals like Saunders, other factors intervened. Once the project began and teachers appeared for training it was evident that consideration beyond support for the program had affected the participation of schools and teachers. The length of time since a school had participated in a staff development project was apparently a factor in selection even though it had nothing to do with commitment to the writing program.

"Those that hadn't had such a project recently were given priority whether or not they were committed to the teaching of writing," said an observer familiar with the selection process. "One school that was very committed to writing was bypassed because it had had a staff development project recently. Another school was included because of the pressure of parents who wanted the school to do more with writing. But what the parents wanted was organization and mechanics, not the kind of creative writing in this program. Nonetheless, the school was chosen, the teachers felt very estranged from the program, and the principal remained uninvolved."

Alexs Pate, one of those hired to work with teachers as a Writer in Residence, found some teachers so lacking in enthusiasm that they struck him as having been conscripted for the project, though the administration insisted they were volunteers. "Some didn't want anything to do with the program and were downright hostile to it," Pate said. "But I didn't mind their attitude because my energy was tuned into trying to convert them and some started coming around."

The Achievements from Outside

Whatever the motivation of the participants, regardless of the city, the goal was to enhance the teaching profession by giving teachers more respectability, authority, and status. The amenities, the recognition, the opportunities for colleagueship with people in higher education and business — all were incentives that distinguished the program and made it attractive to teachers. What school systems conducting the usual in-service programs, without such amenities, seem not to realize is that the attempt to confer knowledge in a setting without dignity is frequently counterproductive. Teachers don't have to be sent to tropical islands to be given information under palm trees, as is done in some of the professions, but neither should they have to do it after a full day's work, in a dingy room without so much as a cup of coffee.

"At a time that teachers are on the firing line and being told that they are doing things all wrong, a time when they are told they are not the cream of the crop, along comes an organization that says it will recognize that you are an intelligent being and will give you funding to carry out some of your ideas," said Barbara van Ausdall, a teacher in St. Louis, who approves heartily of CHART.

The Collaboratives for Humanities and Arts Teaching took a different form in each city, and there was no single model espoused as the only way to work with teachers. It did not matter whether it was an outside organization or the school system itself overseeing the project. What the programs generally had in common was an approach that brought teachers together in groups at sites away from the schools to pursue joint enterprises. In the best of circumstances they were paid to meet during the summer and were released from duties to collaborate during the regular school year. The diversity of the program was illustrated by its scope, which usually included seminars during the summer, institutes during the school year, and gatherings with college professors, businesspeople, and representatives of cultural institutions.

Teachers in St. Louis participated in the program run by the International Educational Consortium, an outside organization, to help teachers of all subjects integrate material on international issues into the curriculum. The most obvious participants were teachers of literature, social studies, and foreign languages, but also involved were teachers of business education, home economics, and other subjects in which the curriculum could be reshaped to include more teaching about the rest of the world.

Crossroads Seattle had a similar purpose: to develop international themes and multicultural perspectives in the curriculum. One of its first thrusts was to help ninth-grade social studies teachers revamp the world history curriculum to reflect more than the Western European heritage that was so prominent a feature.

The Los Angeles Educational Partnership used its grant from the Rockefeller Foundation for a program it named Humanitas. As its first venture, Humanitas sought to promote the development of interdisciplinary teaching. Teams of teachers representing several subject areas were brought together within a select set of high schools to study, do research, confer with each other, and meet with university scholars to plan interdisciplinary courses in their home schools.

A main activity supported with Rockefeller money in Philadelphia was the writing across the curriculum project. The Philadelphia Alliance worked with the school district to train teachers to increase the frequency and quality of their students' writing, the quality and effectiveness of writing assignments, and the use of writing as a teaching method in all subjects.

In New York, an organization known as Global Perspectives in Education brought ninth-grade social studies teachers together from twelve secondary schools to deepen their knowledge of subject matter and to work on curriculum development in the face of a new state-mandated requirement in world history.

The school system itself in Pittsburgh strove to move courses away from the lecture method of teaching and increase the amount of informed, productive discussions that took place in classes. This meant working with teachers on their teaching techniques, developing tests that assessed students on their ability to think critically rather than their familiarity with facts, and making a special effort to infuse arts courses with discussion of ideas instead of relying solely on studio performance.

All of the high schools in Atlanta formed teams of from two to four members to participate in the program that was run by the National Faculty. Teachers were drawn from English, social studies, foreign languages, and fine arts, and each team collaborated with a faculty member from one of the universities in the Atlanta area to plan programs and bring in speakers to deal with topics of interest to the teachers.

The South Carolina Humanities Initiative was devoted to cultivating the use of computers for improving the reading and writing of high school students in rural regions of the state. And, as was mentioned, Saint Paul's program centered on improving writing in the schools.

In almost every participating city, CHART was just one of a variety of activities offered by the outside organization. The agencies in both Philadelphia and Los Angeles, for instance, have extensive programs of minigrants, small competitive awards made directly to teachers and groups of teachers to enable them to carry out projects of their own design. In some cities, there are also programs through which the outside organizations work with groups of mathematics or science teachers, reaching beyond the teachers in the humanities who are the primary beneficiaries of the program sponsored by the Rockefeller Foundation. What is important for purposes of this book is that many of the same principles are at work in other programs, regardless of the funding source. The objective is to enhance the position of teachers, propelling them down the road toward empowerment.

Ideally, the teachers involved in such programs work together, and the bonds of collegiality that develop are of the sort seldom nurtured in the typical school. This kind of experience, reminiscent of the Advanced Management Program at Harvard, where senior business executives live and study together over the summer, can forge ties strong enough to link people for the length of their careers. It is a vital networking element that usually is not part of professional development programs for teachers. Such an approach was a feature of CHART, succeeding beyond anyone's grandest hopes in some instances and at other times having a less lasting effect than an encounter at a cocktail party. But the idea of organizing teachers around intellectual goals that they could pursue in a supportive climate was certainly a first step toward dispelling feelings of powerlessness.

2 ▶▶

STATUS

ANY EFFORT to upgrade teaching must begin with improving the circumstances of teachers so that they can feel better about themselves and what they do for a living. Money is mentioned most frequently in such discussions, and it is not an insignificant factor in boosting teacher morale, but the working conditions that lead teachers to the depths of despair are no less important. Enhancing their status is a first step toward empowerment because so long as teachers are undervalued by themselves and others they are not likely to feel they have much power.

The lack of standing takes many annoying forms for teachers. Bonnie Davis, a teacher at Oakville High School in Melville, a St. Louis suburb, for instance, remembers the day her principal, whom she had always addressed as "Doctor" even though they were about the same age, invited her to call him by his first name. It came after Davis, who had been working at the high school for many years, had gained more confidence and had finally started asserting herself professionally. "I think he saw me in a new way," she said of her principal.

There is, of course, a good deal more to achieving success as a teacher than being permitted to call the boss by his or her first name, but it captures the essence of the problem for teachers, who, as a group, have come to feel small and insignificant about a job they think is not adequately appreciated. Empowerment depends very much on lifting their status. Doing something about status is implied in the elements cited in *Horace's Compromise* (Sizer, 1984) as those that our culture uses to signal respect: autonomy, money, and recognition. Those who see themselves as having less worth than others are not likely to feel a sense of authority about what they do. Any program intended to make teachers more powerful must address the need to raise them up as people and as professionals. Thus, while it may be more difficult to provide teachers with salaries of the size that would assure them of greater respect in a society that seems to value money more highly than intellect or sacrifice, it certainly would cost less to increase the amount of autonomy and recognition given to teachers.

It is fashionable to ascribe the current low status of teachers to the social upheaval of the last generation, but a glimpse of how teachers have been treated through the generations shows that they have always occupied the role of underlings: "Self-denial was the sine qua non of a school teacher's life. It was a prudish existence not far removed from that of the men of an earlier era who arrived penniless in the New World as indentured servants, obligated to teach children of the landed gentry in exchange for their eventual freedom. Josiah Royce, the philosopher, wrote in 1883 that a teacher might find 'that his non-attendance in church, or the fact that he drinks beer with his lunch, or rides a bicycle is considered of more moment than his powers to instruct.' One can almost visualize those risqué teachers, taking clandestine spins on their satanic bicycles. It was not until more than half-way through the twentieth century that teachers began to shake free of the rigid codes of conduct imposed on them by school boards and administrators. One teacher, Minnich Revonna, remembered that when she started teaching in a small Oklahoma town in the mid-1950's she was told where to live, not to use tobacco or alcohol, not to get involved in politics, and to attend church regularly. Add the bicycle restriction and it might as well have been the teacher whom Royce was describing three-quarters of a century earlier" (Maeroff, 1982, pp. 160–61).

The sad fact is that for most of its practitioners teaching is an occupation with few amenities. Just giving teachers business cards to hand out was enough to win goodwill for one of the programs of CHART. With that one act — something taken for granted by most professionals — the program conferred a kind of dignity that the teachers never before had enjoyed.

What teachers must tolerate was illustrated in one city participating in CHART, where they complained about not having enough books to distribute one to each student. In Seattle, Sarah Kaplan had to tape black paper over the windows of her classroom each time she wanted to show a film because she was unable to get the request filled that she made continually for window shades. Worse than that, in New York City until just a few years ago, the people who repaired the window shades were paid more than the new teachers. New York is also the place where overcrowding at Public School 47 in the Bronx made it necessary for a teacher of English as a second language to hold her classes in one of the bathrooms because no other space was made available to her. When New York City teachers were asked by their union to fill out questionnaires in anticipation of the contract negotiations in 1987, morale was the area in which most suggestions were offered for the bargainers to take to the table.

While professionals in other fields are used to being treated to lunch and taking others to lunch, teachers hardly ever get so much as a free cup of coffee. Expense accounts are the exotica of another planet. Teachers in New York City even have to punch time clocks as if they worked on an assembly line in a factory. In Chicago, where there are no time clocks, they sign in and out in log books in the school's main office, a procedure not unusual around the country. "Impotence is a good word to describe the teaching profession," said Jerry Simpson, an elementary school teacher in Saint Paul.

For people supposedly trained to perform a very specific task, teachers spend a good part of their time doing work for which the taxpayers would be better off hiring paraprofessionals. The culture or milieu of the school itself is very much part of the problem. Uplifting teachers and empowering them depends very much on changing the atmosphere in schools. This is not easy. Few other professionals or aspiring professionals spend their workday with children. Few others must deal with a constituency — parents, taxpayers, school board members, lawmakers — all of whom have been through the process and think they know something about it. Few others work a full-time job that many outsiders view as part-time employment because of the vacation schedule. Few others must attend to so much busywork that is not intrinsic to the main task.

Between 10 and 50 percent of a teacher's time is spent on noninstructional duties — recording test scores, monitoring the halls and the playgrounds, running copying machines (Carnegie Forum, 1986, p. 15). On top of these indignities teachers often do not even have the bare essentials they need to do their work. "They are constantly running out of supplies, forced to use outdated texts and make do with inadequate materials," the report of the Carnegie Forum Task Force said. "Skilled support help is rarely available, nor the time to do the job right" (p. 15). Can you imagine engineers being asked to do their jobs without calculators, or accountants being told that they have used up their quota of ledgers for the month? "In sum," according to Ernest L. Boyer, "the teacher's world is often frustrating, frequently demeaning and sometimes dangerous" (1983). It is hardly a desirable job description.

Such nonprofessional demands on their time have helped drive more than one good teacher out of the business. Martha Fiske, for instance, gave up a job in Wellesley, Massachusetts at one of the most elite public high schools in the country because she had had enough.

Though she was high on the pay scale and had visited the White House as a "distinguished teacher," she told Robert Marquand of the *Christian Science Monitor* that it was impossible to do an adequate job of teaching with the large class load assigned to her and the many out-of-class duties she had to perform. "If you want me to be a professional and publish articles on *King Lear*, don't ask me to pick up litter in the girls' room or catch potato puffs on lunch duty," Fiske said. "Why not hire minimum-wage people? Isn't it counterproductive to pay someone $36,000 to supervise a bathroom?" (1986).

On top of other indignities, teachers are infantilized, transformed into adult workers who sometimes have an almost parent–child relationship with their principals. "Teachers are used to being led by the hand and told what to do," said Dee Pinkerton, who began teaching in Seattle in 1957. Such treatment of teachers runs counter to what psychologists say is an important component of good mental health, namely, the sense of being in control of one's destiny. If anything, psychologists are more convinced than ever of the need for workers to feel they have some control over their jobs.

Matters have been made worse for teachers by the instability that has been added to teaching since the 1970s. Before that, teaching was at least a secure job; it did not pay well, but the position was there as long as the teacher wanted it. No more. A new word has entered the vocabulary of American teachers: rif. It is the acronym for the dreaded "reduction in force" that has led to some teachers getting fired to keep a school district within its budget. The horror of riffing is that some younger teachers have had to endure it year after year, getting dismissed each June and hired again in September — having no assurance in June that there will be a job in September. "The uncertainty of it all makes you feel like a vagabond," said Jack Rousso, a Seattle teacher who has been riffed about a half-dozen times in 14 years. "You feel you have an adverse relationship with your employer. A lot of teachers get to feeling like outsiders."

Ronald Richardson, a 37-year-old Los Angeles foreign language teacher who has worked in nursery school, elementary school, and high school, felt so discouraged by what he saw that he considered leaving teaching: "You go into the cafeteria and have lunch each day with people who are tired-looking and very hesitant to take on any new responsibilities. They are bogged down by details and when we get together the only sharing is to ridicule the students. There are a lot of things that are real turnoffs. There is an older teacher who even prides himself on being a bigot. People in teaching seem very unwilling to accept new ideas and are resentful of anyone telling them what to do.

They are negative. They don't welcome an interchange of ideas. There is almost never a discussion of what worked in the classroom. People don't share their successes, maybe because there are so few of them. Isolation is a real problem for teachers. It leads to alienation and causes people to leave the profession. Some seem to be just waiting to retire. They say they would never encourage their students or their own children to go into teaching. There is not great support for the profession. But teachers want to feel that they are doing a good job; they want to be liked by their students and respected by other adults. There is a hunger for professional contacts and for sharing."

The isolation Richardson mentioned is a main problem in schoolteaching. Many teachers work an entire day without contact with a colleague except over lunch, which often turns out to be the only setting in which pent-up frustrations can be vented. "You tend to become exceedingly isolated in your school and in your school system," according to Jim Wiswall of Northwest High School in St. Louis. "Your entire focus becomes limited to your problems at school and your problems at home and you can go insane. You get to feeling you are a nerd."

THE CURSE OF ISOLATION

Teaching is what Al Saunders, a principal in Saint Paul, calls "the most secret profession" because, he said, a long time passes without any other adult seeing what is going on behind the closed doors. Dale Mann, a professor at Teachers College of Columbia University, suggests that teacher morale could be raised and isolation diminished simply by installing a telephone in each teacher's classroom, an idea so fundamental and practical that almost no school district has done it. Imagine a teacher who is trying a new approach being able to ring up a colleague and ask for a moment of advice.

Sally Flood, who has spent 14 years in the Seattle public schools, thinks the isolation and alienation bring out the worst instincts in teachers. "In my building," she said, "we do not share achievements or knowledge, even in department meetings. What we share are gripes and disappointments. We have to deal with professional jealousies. When we talk it is about each other: gossip."

Teachers, separated as they are in their classrooms, normally have little time to share and compare ideas. Professional growth is bound to be impaired in a setting where practitioners, in this case teachers, do not see their colleagues practice their profession and hardly ever teach each other techniques. What a difference, for example, from a team of lawyers who prepare a case together or a group of surgeons who confer about how to handle a medical procedure.

The organizational structure of schools, so far as the professional staff is concerned, is built on a series of one-to-one relationships. Since there is little incentive for teachers to integrate their behavior with that of other teachers, they tend to go their own ways. Often, this pattern is reinforced by the principal, who mostly deals with teachers individually and gives little attention "to organizational norms or improving the functioning of the school as an organization" (Jwaideh, 1984).

Teachers are so accustomed to working on their own that they are taken by surprise when someone tries to act as a colleague and collaborate. Roseanne Lloyd, a Minnesota author, found teachers suspicious of her when she was first assigned through CHART to work in a school in Saint Paul as a Writer in Residence whose job was to help teachers in their teaching of writing. "They couldn't believe that someone would be their ally," Lloyd observed. "They didn't believe that I meant it when I said, 'Tell me what you want me to do for you.' No one asks them that. They were so happy to get validation for the good things they were doing. They normally get very little recognition. There are people in the school so isolated that they don't even trust anyone else on the faculty." Being so isolated that they get little feedback, teachers end up dwelling on the limitations of the job and their own shortcomings, saying they have no sense that anyone really cares about them or what they are doing.

Bringing Teachers Together

Ending their sense of isolation and helping teachers feel they are part of something greater seems essential. The beginning of the end of isolation is bringing teachers together, as was done in connection with CHART in many cities. Teachers feel more powerful when they are part of a group with a common purpose than when they labor on their own. Coming together to work on a project with other teachers who share their dedication and conscientiousness is a pleasant awakening. "The isolation of the classroom is overwhelming and the real benefit of this [CHART] is as an affirmation of the value of what I am doing," Clinton Blandford of Lindbergh High School, outside St. Louis, said of his opportunity to come together with other teachers in CHART. "Otherwise, without this kind of contact, I don't know if I am really in touch."

One of the best efforts at putting teachers in touch with each other is Impact II, a program that began in New York City and Houston and then spread across the country to almost two dozen other districts to allow teachers to share their good ideas with other teachers. First, the teachers compete for awards to put their ideas into practice, and then they are plugged into an apparatus that allows them to disseminate the innovations. The teacher originating the idea gets a $300 developer grant to implement it; then other teachers get $200 adapter grants to replicate it. Catalogues and brochures are published with the ideas of Impact II teachers and information on how the teacher originating the idea can be contacted. There are local and national meetings, and Impact II even provides funds so that teachers can be released to go to schools and meetings to demonstrate their innovations. For instance, Olive Tomlinson, a reading teacher in Brooklyn, developed what she named "The Fairy Tale Kit." It is a program that teachers can use to help students gain a background in fairy tale literature, learn the key elements in the construction of a fairy tale, and, eventually, write their own fairy tales.

"There not only is a sense of professionalism about it, but it also gives you credibility as a teacher," said Patricia Suarez Weiss, an elementary school Spanish teacher in Manhattan whose Impact II project enables Spanish to be introduced to first graders through puppets and games. "You know that what you are doing is right and appropriate and that it is something to be shared. This produces a permanent networking system so that you are no longer just isolated and doing your own thing."

One vital accomplishment of CHART, just as in Impact II, was the building of an esprit de corps among teachers. This was helped by the fact that teachers, during the training, were removed from the school setting, something like going on a retreat and spending several weeks working together. They collaborated in ways they never did on the job. They got to know each other in a new light and the bonds they forged seemed strong enough to link them throughout the school year. Since there are so few opportunities for teachers to interact on a deep level with other teachers, the projects made a great contribution by weaving strands to connect teachers.

One cannot overemphasize the importance of giving teachers a chance to get out of the school building. They almost never travel out of town in conjunction with their work, as many professionals do; it seems to take a dispensation from headquarters just to enable them to leave their building during the day to attend a local professional conference. "The best person in the world can be speaking somewhere during the school day but you can't hear him if your school district isn't willing to arrange for you to be able to go," said Sarah Kaplan, who said she was so distant from power that her participation in CHART marked the first time in her 20 years in the Seattle school system that she was part of a curriculum-writing project.

The Barriers to Getting Together

School systems are hard-pressed financially and must set priorities for expenditures. It is not surprising that conference money is scarce, but it is just one more symbol of low status to teachers. "Having the flexibility to leave the building and go to meetings is very important," said Bill Hampton, a former high school principal who became assistant to the superintendent in the Ferguson-Florrisant District outside St. Louis. "It gives more dignity to what they are doing. The ability of administrators to control their own time makes teachers jealous."

Bringing teachers into closer contact with one another is a key to moving them closer to empowerment. The way that schools are structured seems to conspire against collegiality and the empowerment it can produce. The less that they deal with each other, the more teachers are likely not to trust one another. The person in the next room — potentially a colleague — is, instead, a competitor.

The extent of the division among teachers and what can happen when finally they are brought together was illustrated when a team leader of a CHART project in one city approached the program with trepidation because of the composition of his team. It included two teachers from opposite political extremes who often gossiped about each other. But each was hard working, and they were the first two at the school who, separately, approached him to ask if they could join the team. "I worried that having these two on the team would mean that nothing would get done, that we would just have disagreements all the time," the team leader said. "But now that they have spent a summer together they are cordial to each other. Each has privately told me of the respect he has developed for the other. This simply doesn't happen in the normal school setting. I think we can build on this experience back in school. We will try to bring the experience into other departments and try to affect collegiality throughout the school."

One reason that more isn't done to help teachers make allies of each other is that some principals do not go out of their way to encourage it. Only principals confident about themselves are apt to try to end isolation among teachers. Principals who are insecure are not likely to encourage interaction among teachers for fear that teachers will unite against them. Caught in this kind of bind, many teachers retreat inward. An example is an experienced math teacher at John Adams High

School in Cleveland, who was asked to join the board of the city's Urban Mathematics Collaborative. He accepted but sat silently at meetings, deferring to other board members who were school administrators, college professors, and business executives. Finally, having gained experience at being something more than a sole practitioner in an isolated classroom, he blossomed through the activities of the Collaborative. He ended up speaking to groups on behalf of the Collaborative, editing the newsletter, writing letters to the editor of the local newspaper, and being nominated for a Teacher of the Year award.

LIFTING SPIRITS

Teachers say they can draw new strength from each other. For instance, Kathryn Symmes, an English teacher at Thomas Jefferson High School in Los Angeles, felt much stronger because of the interaction she had with colleagues in CHART. "This program is good because at least we get respect from our colleagues for our knowledge and we respect each other and are inspired by each other's knowledge," she said. "You get to think that teachers may be okay." Such interaction also allows teachers to feel that someone has confidence in their abilities. Thus, Jan Maher, an art teacher in Seattle, welcomed the opportunity to work on curriculum development because it showed her "that someone trusts teachers to have expertise."

Liz Woods in Philadelphia said that as the result of the PATHS program, which allowed teachers to work together during the summer and continue their association during the school year, faculty members who participated were more unified and identified more closely with each other. "Because you have something to share, you become colleagues instead of fellow victims," she said. "In a big city system teachers are getting screwed all the time and a lot of teacher gatherings focus only on this. By sharing a good experience and gaining unity you feel proud and that empowers you. It is a real high." Dignity is what teachers covet.

Getting to know one another also helps teachers rid themselves of stereotypes about each other. There is a pecking order, however tacit, in education, in which college teachers look down on high school teachers, high school teachers look down on junior high school teachers, and junior high school teachers look down on elementary school teachers. At one gathering of Ford's Urban Math Collaborative in Los Angeles, following a presentation by a professor from California Institute of Technology, some of the high school teachers — who did not have a good grasp of the subject—were dumbstruck by the penetrating question asked by a junior high school math teacher. "Yes, that's another way of looking at it," the professor conceded to the junior high school teacher, whose incisiveness raised his stature in the minds of the high school teachers.

Teachers in the programs sponsored by Rockefeller and Ford were not simply the passive recipients of lectures. They usually had to make contributions of their own. In some cases this meant developing a curriculum to use alone or in a team-teaching situation once back in school. The process by which this teaching material was developed could be seen one summer morning in the Marshall School in Seattle, for example, where teachers in CHART had broken into small groups to develop different portions of a new world history curriculum. In one classroom, four teachers, mostly dressed in jeans and T-shirts, were trying to fashion a unit in which they would focus on social order in society as a way to teach about India and China. The guiding question by which they gauged the appropriateness of the material they were writing was: What does it tell about how a society creates its cultural traditions?

All of a sudden one of the teachers called a halt in the deliberations and said to his colleagues: "I have a burning question. What is the relevance of all this so far as the students are concerned?"

"They will have to learn that these cultures are of this world and they ought to know how they evolved," answered one of the other teachers.

"We're talking here about the two most populated countries in the world," interjected another of the teachers, "and so if you want to know about other people in the world this is the place to start. After all, they do make up about 40 percent of the world's population."

And so it went as they debated and agonized each step of the way, deciding which aspect of Chinese or Indian society must be included in the curriculum if students were to be led into a fruitful examination of how social order is achieved, maintained, and lost. It was an arduous journey, but clearly it provided the teachers with the kind of exhiliration that made them feel better about being teachers.

Such experiences enabled many teachers around the country to go back to their own schools and to other schools as well to help fellow teachers learn what they had learned. The approach is formulated on the assumption that teachers have something to contribute. They learn from each other, seeing, firsthand, what their colleagues have to give. For many it was their first time interacting with fellow teachers as colleagues trying to grow together.

Teachers found their spirits lifted. One in Los Angeles checked out

10 books at a time from the library, hardly able to wait to put into practice what she had learned. "I am inspired in a way that I never was before and I finally feel good about myself as a teacher," she said. Two teachers in Philadelphia and another in St. Louis were inspired to enter doctoral programs in the humanities. "I feel better about myself," said Stephanie Maupin, a suburban St. Louis teacher. One of the teams that participated in the program in Los Angeles saved money that had been paid from the program for their own use and pooled it when they returned to their school to buy materials and pay for field trips for students. Elsewhere, some teachers wrote of their experiences and presented the papers at academic conferences.

A sense of community can be fostered among teachers in such situations. What added to their enthusiasm in the Collaboratives for Humanities and Arts Teaching and in similar ventures was the fact that they attended as volunteers. They were not required to participate as is so often the case with inservice education programs after school or the college courses teachers must take to accumulate credits for raises. The voluntary aspect added further luster when the number of applicants exceeded the number of positions and teachers were chosen, singled out because of their promise. Teachers, after all, are in a business in which most of the structures do not give them opportunity for individual recognition.

In part, the failure to feel a sense of specialness is something teachers have brought on themselves through collective bargaining contracts that require people to be treated the same even when some are clearly more able than others. There are readily understandable reasons why teachers in the last 25 years have gravitated toward collective bargaining and the protection it affords. But they have paid a price in loss of individuality, becoming part of a cookie-cutter operation. If all the gingerbread figures are made to look alike on the outside even though they are of different consistency on the inside, chances are diminished of their gaining the individual attention they may deserve.

Unlike many kinds of volunteers, the teachers were paid for their time through CHART, though they say the symbol of the money was more important than the income. "I didn't do it for the money," said Pat Cygan in Seattle. "It empowers teachers by letting them be active, effective participants in school management. That counts for more than the money."

Carol Olson, an elementary school teacher in Saint Paul, got a lift just in being tapped to participate in the writing program that the outside organization, Compas, made available to teachers. "By giving me this opportunity the school system is finally saying to me that what I do is important," Olson said. "I would be grateful to have a pat on the back once in a while, but the system has never given me that feeling before. I'm not asked at what point certain things should be taught and I'm told the sequence in which to teach concepts even though sometimes what they are telling me goes against what Piaget said children are ready for developmentally. The most appreciated I ever felt was a few years ago when the parents of some of my students nominated me for teacher of the year. It made me feel appreciated. Teachers would feel more empowered and not burn out as fast if more happened to make them feel valued."

A Boost by Higher Education and Business

Teachers know that someone is concerned about their well-being when they get plaudits and recognition from the outside. This was built into CHART—working better in some instances than in others. An important element in this respect was the involvement of universities and business corporations. The outside contact with professors and business-people opened another window to the world for the teachers. Such contacts can have an impact on the way teachers see themselves. "You get the idea that they regard you as a professional and that you are worthy of being exposed to experts," Barbara Vires said of the university professors that the St. Louis teachers got to know informally as well as formally. "If you feel you are respected and are paid a decent salary you'll do a better job. You'll feel that you are valued."

Looking at the effect that the project had on teachers in Los Angeles, Dan Isaacs, an assistant superintendent, marveled at how much it meant to teachers to be invited to the campus of the University of Southern California in connection with CHART in that city and to be treated in first-class style. "It means increased status for teachers," Isaacs said. "When the teachers went to USC, they felt good about being there. The fact that they were having drinks and dinner at Town and Gown [the club on campus] at a prestigious university meant a lot to them. Doing this through LAEP [Los Angeles Educational Partnership] is a way of bringing status to teachers. Anything we can do to enhance the perception of the teacher in the community is valuable."

The potential for boosting the status of schoolteachers through associations with higher education is exquisitely illustrated by the Yale–New Haven Teachers Institute, which has been a national model since its inception in 1978. Though not part of CHART, it has received support from the Foundation as well as from the National Endowment for the Humanities and other foundations. Teachers in the New Haven public schools have had the opportunity to take seminars that the university puts together just for the teachers. Senior professors on the faculty lead the seminars, which are devoted to topics determined in consultation with the teachers, who are expected to use the time to develop curriculum units in consultation with the professors. And beyond the learning, this is what the New Haven program does for status: "Program participants, who are called 'fellows,' have the opportunity to become members of the university community. They are listed in the Yale directory and enjoy privileges in the libraries and other facilities. This, of course, is no small matter for public school teachers, so many of whom around the country have been conditioned to a professional life in which the amenities are so few that a free cup of coffee is a valued perquisite. For their participation in the program, the teachers are paid a $650 stipend. A poll of New Haven teachers who have been fellows at Yale through the Institute revealed that, for almost half of them, the chance to participate in the program has been an important factor in deciding to remain a public school teacher in New Haven" (Maeroff, 1983, p. 37).

Somewhat similar benefits are available when the right kinds of matches are made between teachers and people in the business world. The contact that teachers in many of the project cities had with cooperating corporations gave them a lift. Being invited to corporate offices to meet with executives and dine with them was a new experience for teachers. "What they have done for us has usually been done with such good taste and class. People in industry make us feel valued," said Marie T. Collins, a Los Angeles teacher. Teachers also said that the involvement of business and industry in supporting the outside agencies that were overseeing CHART in most cities lent credibility to the venture.

The Salary Issue

Such recognition is invaluable in giving teachers the confidence to become more assertive. It is one thing to tolerate onerous conditions if the pay is worthwhile, but teachers have not had even this satisfaction. Treated like peasants and paid like members of a religious order, teachers have received little to offset the disadvantages. On the other hand, there has been a tendency to ascribe too much of the problem of low status to the meager salary level. While higher pay for teachers is certainly desirable, much more than low pay keeps good people away from teaching and drives veterans out of the business. The job itself is simply perceived as undesirable. Money alone, especially considering that it is never likely to be all that much, is not going to get teachers to like themselves and their jobs better. Nor will it assure those getting riffed periodically that their positions will be more stable.

There are factors at least as important as salary in enhancing the attractiveness of schoolteaching. Frederick Herzberg's research on motivation showed that to be inspired in their jobs, whatever their salaries and job security, employees need significance in their work, achievement, recognition, increased responsibilities, and advancement (1966, 1968). Commenting on these findings and similar ones from more recent studies that have concentrated on teachers, Richard P. DuFour, a high school principal in Illinois, wrote: "The implication for a principal seeking to motivate staff members seems clear—simply give teachers more freedom in what they teach and how they teach it and watch their morale improve" (1986).

The fact is that some other fields that pay no better than public school teaching seem to have far less of a problem filling positions. Among newspaper reporters, for example, the average starting salary in 1987 was not much different than in teaching: $19,344 for those at union papers and closer to $12,000 for the vast majority of reporters, who are not at union newspapers. The average pay for experienced reporters at union papers was $31,402; for experienced nonunionized reporters it was not much different from the $26,704 national average for all teachers.

The top salary in early 1987 of $40,950 in New York City for a teacher with 15 years of service and 30 credits beyond a master's degree exceeded the top of the scale at every unionized daily newspaper in the country except the dailies in New York City and a handful of other papers. Thus, the typical reporter or copy editor in the United States could swap positions with a teacher and take home a paycheck of about the same size. Yet, candidates for newspaper jobs, even at the smallest, worst-paying newspapers, are plentiful. They are lured, of course, not by the meager salaries but by the satisfaction of the work and the recognition and influence they can attain.

This sort of comparison is not limited to fields outside teaching. Even many private schools, which usually pay lower salaries than the big city systems, are besieged by job applicants, many with liberal arts degrees from leading colleges. And certainly colleges and universities, which in general pay faculty members on a par with those who work in the schools—the average faculty salary in higher education in 1986–87 was $35,470—has no shortage of candidates for positions. Thus, improving working conditions and the trappings of teaching is crucial to making teaching in public schools more desirable. Attesting to this is the finding of Berry (1986) that the brightest college seniors not studying education say that the most significant reasons they are not considering teaching relate not to the pay but to frustrating working conditions, bureaucratic requirements, the lack of professional control, and the limited opportunities for intellectual growth.

All of this, of course, is not meant in any way to justify the low salaries in education. There are some very fundamental questions to ask about a society in which an advertiser pays $1 million a minute to put a commercial on television during football's Super Bowl, a sum that would pay the salaries of 40 teachers for a year.

More Than Money

In the absence of higher salaries, at least paying attention to people and recognizing their achievements can make them feel more valued. "It is real easy to stagnate in the city system," said Margaret Campbell of Northwest High School in St. Louis. That is why the intervention of an activity like CHART, with the sort of recognition it gave teachers, made Campbell feel better about being a teacher. She said: "This regenerates me and makes me want to do something besides take the easy way out. It gives me a chance to talk to other teachers and get positive reinforcement." Some teachers valued themselves in ways that they had not experienced since their earliest days in teaching. This is no small matter and it is certainly a step toward improving the schools and giving a better education to the students. People who don't think much of themselves are not likely to think much of others, especially those who are less powerful than they — their students.

Nina Wasserman, an elementary school teacher in New York, felt she could "make a difference" after her work was recognized by Impact II. "These little rewards are necessary to keep a teacher going," she said. "You need encouragement and recognition. You have to know that you're not a jerk, like some people would have you believe, that you are doing something valuable."

Even the trappings can be used to uplift teachers, as was seen in CHART. Unlike the drab classrooms to which they are accustomed, the sites for conferences and workshops sponsored by CHART often enhanced the teachers' sense of importance. They felt elite and pampered. In Philadelphia, for example, sessions met at such stately places as the Rosenbach Museum and Library, a brownstone on one of the city's most exclusive streets; the Historical Society of Pennsylvania, a research facility used by scholars and filled with the portraits of the city's founding fathers; the Independence Hall complex with its eighteenth-century flavor; the Atwater Kent Museum, a place of imposing columns that contains artifacts of the city's history; the Philadelphia Museum of Art, a Parthenon-like building with a sweeping view of the city; and the University Museum of the University of Pennsylvania, one of the world's great archaeological museums right in the middle of an Ivy League campus. "There has been a sense of class and good taste to the whole thing," said Albert I. Glassman, superintendent of one of the subdistricts into which the Philadelphia school system is divided.

The transformation in the attitude of teachers was remarkable in one of the more troubled school systems in which CHART operated. People who had despaired suddenly felt hopeful. People whose morale was broken felt somewhat restored. The teachers who developed a new curriculum found an outlet for enthusiasm they did not know was still inside of them. They met daily with fellow teachers, arguing about fine points and finding themselves stimulated by the encounters, after so many years of ennui. And, they thought, if their school system didn't care about what they were doing, at least they know they cared about each other.

Such an experience can be liberating. The Task Force of the Carnegie Forum said in its report that teachers should have more authority for what occurs in schools. A first step in this direction is surely to give teachers greater autonomy. Inevitably, such control will lead them to feel they have some power over the circumstances of their professional lives. This has to be part of what professionalization of teaching means. After all, those who are members of a profession are people who are not simply at the beck and call of others. "The real key in all this is the autonomy you're given to do the job in a professional way," Clinton Blandford of St. Louis said.

It is through involvement in curriculum planning and policy making that teachers can "become valued and contributing members of the faculty and of their profession" (Presseisen, 1985). The point was reinforced by identifying characteristics common in the treatment of teachers in the half-dozen "good" high schools, particularly the centrality of the decision-making role accorded to teachers at those schools (Lightfoot, 1983). Lightfoot wrote: "The teachers in these schools are recognized as the critical educational authorities; the ones who will guide the learning, growth and development of students. . . . They give shape to what is taught, how it is taught and in what context it is transmitted" (pp. 333–34). Her description of Highland Park High School outside Chicago illustrated the point in its portrayal of a school in which teachers, who were recognized as intellectuals, were responsible for designing and shaping the curriculum with few directions sent from above (pp. 121–49).

If teachers are treated in ways that cause them to have this sort of vision of the schools in which they work, then they will be inspired to become active believers in the possibilities of empowerment. A teacher like Ronald Richardson in Los Angeles, who had been thinking about leaving the field before he got involved in CHART, ended up reevaluating his once-dire outlook. "I still may leave but I don't think about it as much anymore," he said. "I'm starting to feel like I can make a difference. I want to be one of the best teachers these kids have ever had, but that's not easy."

3 ►►

KNOWLEDGE

BEING A SCHOOLTEACHER is having so much to do and so little time to do it that keeping up with the growth in knowledge is a luxury. Even the most dedicated teacher finds that trying to stay abreast of subject matter is like paddling upstream on a fast-moving river. For the typical high school teacher, meeting with 125 to 175 students a day, marking many of the papers at night, and preparing for the next day's classes — not to mention maintaining a family life and possibly a part-time job — it is a task without beginning or end.

"Bells are always ringing and you're running back and forth," said Shahdia Khan, an English teacher at Ingraham High School in Seattle. "You get a half-hour for lunch and there's no time to interact professionally with your colleagues. There is just some bitching about the administrators and everyone talking about how frustrated they are. When school is over you're so tired you don't want to talk to anyone."

Much of the criticism directed at teachers in recent years has been aimed at alleged ineptness, assertions that teachers are ignorant of subject matter and unsuited to impart information to others. The charge is not without basis. Almost every parent seems to have a horror story about a teacher who sends home notes with misspelled words. All too many students have suffered through a year of classes with a teacher who has no business in a classroom.

Strengthening the intellectual and methodological foundation of teachers is one of the most important challenges facing those who want to improve the quality of instruction. Such a change is vital if teaching is to take on a professional aura; for without proficiency at one's craft, there is little hope of exerting authority in the exercise of that craft. "It makes you feel braver and more willing to try things," a St. Louis teacher said of the confidence that her increased knowledge has given her. A stronger and surer knowledge base and a greater command of methodology inevitably contribute to a teacher's power. They lend authority of the sort that allows a person to teach with confidence and to command the respect of students and colleagues. This is not power of the sort that makes people jump when fingers are snapped; rather it is the kind of power that will enhance the education of students coming in contact with such a teacher.

The issue is whether or not teachers have pedagogical authority. All teachers have authority that is given to them to regulate deportment in the classroom and to cover the scope and sequence of the curriculum — in effect, the authority of rules. With the authority of expertise, however, comes the ability "to guard against, and to alert students to, errors and half-truths in texts and prepared curriculum. Such a teacher will have the authority to request and argue for better mathematics books, a more enlightened reader, a less racist social studies book, simply because he or she will know the difference" (Tozer, 1985).

The need for help in keeping up arises shortly after a teacher's career begins; the monumental chores of teaching quickly make someone feel that he or she is falling behind. The longer someone has been teaching, the greater the need for intervention that will update the person. Because of declines in elementary and secondary school enrollments, the nation's teaching force was not augmented in the 1970s and 1980s as it was in the 1950s and 1960s. Thus, there was not an infusion of new blood to keep the average age of teachers young. The graying of America's educators could be seen in a city like Atlanta, where by 1987 the average ages were 41 for teachers, 53 for principals, and 57 for central administrators. Furthermore, according to Regina Johnson, an Atlanta administrator, the teachers tended to teach as they had been taught, which meant modeling one's approach on something learned longer and longer ago.

The ingrained attitudes and behaviors of teachers are not easily overcome. When the Ford Foundation critiqued its Comprehensive School Improvement Program, which invested $30 million in the schools during the 1960s, it found that the most formidable obstacle to improvement of schools was the inadequacies of teachers (*A Foundation Goes to School*, 1972). Continuing education programs were not meeting the need of teachers to grow in their jobs; the introduction of new approaches and new materials was hindered by the inability of teachers to use them, according to the Ford critique, and by the lack of opportunity for them to learn how. Under such conditions, teachers certainly cannot be very powerful in the exercise of their craft.

A difficulty in equipping someone with the knowledge needed to teach has been that, despite a body of courses that masquerade as the essential core of teacher education, there has been disagreement over the elements of that core. And then, as if to further complicate the dispute, those who complete the teacher training programs and go out to teach say after a few years that the courses they took in the methods of teaching were largely a waste of time. It is no wonder that so many teachers feel powerless, having the sense that they were sent into the fray with their hands tied behind their backs, like the young Russians sent to the front without guns by the czar during the First World War. The Holmes Group, the organization of deans from many of the nation's leading colleges of teacher education, issued a reminder in its recent report that competent teaching is a compound of three elements: subject matter knowledge, systematic knowledge of teaching, and reflective practical experience (Holmes Group Report, 1986, p. 62). For those already in the classroom, greater autonomy is likely to come with greater mastery of these three elements.

TRADITIONAL INSERVICE EDUCATION

There are two main ways of retooling and upgrading teachers: inservice instruction and college courses. A third approach, the use of teacher centers, is more recent and still nascent in most places. The fact that the continuing education of teachers persists as a problem shows that none of these methods has proven fully satisfactory.

Inservice education, short-term instruction generally provided at the school itself, is familiar to every teacher, usually in the form of required after-school lectures. Teachers complain that this approach is mechanical and ordinarily deals only with technique, ignoring content. Often, it comes at a point when teachers are so weary they would rather be stretched out on a couch relaxing than sitting upright in a chair trying to concentrate. There is also seldom follow-through to reinforce what was taught.

"The usual inservice is at the end of the day when I've just finished seeing 120 kids; I'm tired and I don't want to be bothered," said Roger Kurtz of Webster Groves High School, outside St. Louis. "One of the worst was one we had recently on how to motivate students and they couldn't even motivate us." Laurence Devine, a social studies department head in a Philadelphia high school, said that inservice tends to be diffuse since it is often aimed at all the teachers in a school rather than focusing on the interests of smaller groups within the faculty. "Inservice or graduate education is often far removed from the classroom and the

speakers don't know what we go through," said Donna Smith of Ritenour High School outside St. Louis.

Furthermore, teachers say inservice just isn't done very well.
"Teachers see inservice as a continuation of methods courses they took in
colleges of education," said Dennis Lubeck, who before becoming head
of CHART in St. Louis was a social studies teacher for 18 years at
suburban University City High School. Methods courses, as almost anyone close to education knows, are regarded with the sort of affection
usually reserved for such alluring activities as a trip to the dentist or an
audit by the IRS. "Inservice tells you things you already know," said
Barbara Vires in St. Louis. "It doesn't deal with content so much as it
does with technique." One school in the St. Louis area, for instance,
recently scheduled a three-part inservice series on how to maintain
discipline in a classroom. At the first session the teachers thought they
learned so little that, in their disappointment, they turned on the lectur-
er with all sorts of hostile questions. "They ate her up," said one of the
participants. The last two sessions were canceled.

Teachers frequently have higher regard for the courses they take as
part-time students at colleges in the evenings, on weekends, and during
the summer than they do for the inservice courses given to them by their
school system in their own schools. But the college courses, even at their
best, cannot provide teachers with some of the advantages they got from
a venture like CHART, which was replete with features usually not
offered in connection with a regular college course.

There is not the same satisfaction in enrolling in a college course
open to anyone willing to pay the tuition as there is in a program where
participants have to be selected. Also, CHART paid stipends to participants, according them the professional recognition to which they were
entitled. Unlike a college course that is fixed in its approach, the content
of the seminars and workshops of CHART was shaped to reflect the
interests and needs of the participants. Because those in the program
were generally all from the same school district and often accompanied
by teams representing schools, the experience of camaraderie was quite
different from sitting in a class—however good it is—with a diverse
group of people who are not colleagues.

In CHART there was, in most cases, year-round follow-up after the
teacher returned to the classroom and a chance for the teacher to be in
the project on an ongoing basis. Teachers have had their fill of one-time
fixes, road shows at which the information is heaped on them and then
the tent is folded, leaving them with nothing to fall back on as they go
off to implement all the wonderful ideas. This can produce frustration
instead of power. Confidence flows from the assurance that there is a

source of continuing support for the teacher, a well from which to draw sustenance when it is available nowhere else. Research shows that teachers view staff development more positively when it is accompanied by a continuing commitment to provide follow-up aid (Daresh, 1987).

Projects that schedule staff meetings frequently and regularly, as most of the cities in CHART tried to do, have fewer implementation problems and greater cohesiveness (McLaughlin, 1978). Where time is given for planning activities as was the objective (not always realized) of the Humanities Program, this can be one of the most important factors contributing to success, according to McLaughlin.

So much for inservice and college courses. The problem with teacher centers is that they simply have not become sufficiently widespread to affect the lives of large numbers of teachers and that where they do exist they often have not fulfilled their potential. Judging by their response to the annual survey of the nation's teachers sponsored by the Metropolitan Life Insurance Company (1986), teachers would welcome a more pervasive presence of teacher centers. When asked about steps that might improve working conditions, 71 percent said that having a formal system of teacher centers where they could get help and ideas from other teachers and administrators would be desirable—the single most cited improvement in working conditions that they mentioned.

What is possible in teacher centers at their best was described in *Teacher Development in Schools* (1985), a report to the Ford Foundation by the Academy for Educational Development: "A dominant theme in teachers' centers was that teachers should control decisions about instruction and that they should also control decisions about their own professional development. . . . The process of information exchange and reflection is the essential stimulant for professional growth. An elemental appeal of teachers' centers is that they provide opportunities for collegial exchange about pedagogy that are rarely encouraged in typically organized and managed schools." No one could fault such an enterprise, but relatively few teachers across the country have had this experience.

A NEW APPROACH TO INSERVICE

There is a desperate need to improve the delivery system for the continuing education of teachers. Without a firmer knowledge base and a better sense of where to turn for information they need, teachers will not have as much control over their professional lives as they might. A look at the projects carried out under the aegis of Rockefeller, Ford, and Carnegie revealed some patterns that hold promise of enabling teachers to go on learning in ways that point toward empowerment. Interviews with participants indicated that the approaches most likely to yield dividends had these characteristics in common.

- Fresh information and new insights.
- Ways to put this knowledge at the disposal of students or at least the opportunity for the time and encouragement to develop those ways.
- The building of an esprit de corps so that teachers, usually in teams, are fired with enthusiasm and not isolated when they return to their schools with new ideas.
- Follow-up mechanisms to lend support to the teachers throughout the school year in implementing the new knowledge and keeping the enthusiasm at a high pitch.

Teachers are hungry for stimulating educational experiences. In CHART and similar programs they said they found intellectual exhiliration of the sort they did not think they could still attain. "Teachers over and over again speak of themselves as 'intellectually starved,' so if you show respect for their minds, they will respond with such enthusiasm that they will knock you down," said Judith Hodgson, head of PATHS in Philadelphia. This wrestling with ideas that they then pulled into their courses was something that many of the teachers said they never before had experienced in continuing professional education. It shows that the whole approach to inservice education must be overhauled if it is to be effective and if teachers are to be equipped with the knowledge and methods of teaching that make them feel empowered.

Margaret Campbell of St. Louis said she was inspired by her week-long experience in CHART over the summer. "I left the workshop with ideas buzzing in my head," she said. "I went home and rewrote my world history curriculum in just a few days. Then, I asked my principal if I could teach it on an experimental basis and he allowed me. I had the best year I have ever had with world history. I didn't teach it chronologically, but by continents. I started with Africa because that's where mankind began and also because it was good for the kids I teach. They are all black. I did Europe last and did the least on it."

It was not Campbell's only inspiration. The same summer, when a rabbi came to the seminar to discuss the Holocaust, she followed him out the door and spoke to him for an hour about his presentation. At her request, the rabbi put Campbell in touch with a concentration camp survivor. That set the stage for her to prepare a unit on the Holocaust for her students. The rabbi came and met with each of four classes to prepare the students for the survivor who was to follow. A few days later all four classes were gathered together in the library to hear the Holocaust survivor.

Five suburban St. Louis teachers in CHART were so inspired by their exposure to the literature and culture of French-speaking West Africa that they eagerly joined a trip to Senegal with the university professor who had lectured to them, a journey that they said in retrospect was a high point of their careers. Bonnie Davis, one of those who went on the trip, said it altered her approach to teaching: "I teach composition to high school students for university credit and I am always looking for topics. I have started focusing units on global perspectives and I got away from textbooks altogether. I designed my own units. In Africa I met writers and university professors."

The route knowledge takes in leading to power was traced through the evolution of a group of Massachusetts teachers whose original purpose in gathering for discussions about educational issues was collegiality for its own sake (McDonald, 1986). "Initially, we had thought it wonderful just to know others who felt the same joys and frustrations in their work that we felt, and to share those joys together and vent those frustrations together," McDonald wrote. "But after a few months of sharing and venting, the wonder wore off, and it seemed that we ought to do something more." The "something more" was using their deeper knowledge of educational theory to gain some power in the school. In the end, they felt that their claim to greater power was strengthened by what they had learned about teaching in applying the theories in their own classrooms.

INTERDISCIPLINARY TEACHING

Finding subjects of common affinity is easier among elementary school teachers, since they all teach all subjects, than it is among the specialists who teach in secondary schools. Sometimes it seems that secondary teachers are as sharply delineated by discipline as those who teach in universities. But one way to bring together secondary teachers — other than delving into teaching methods, a topic that cuts across disciplines — is to encourage them to think about an interdisciplinary curriculum.

In Los Angeles, CHART lent itself easily to the cross-fertilization of ideas since the goal was to write an interdisciplinary curriculum unit.

Teams of teachers from various departments — English, social studies, art — spent the summer together, learning new material and then figuring out how they could blend it. The process was intriguing as it unfolded one morning in the air-conditioned library of a classroom building on the campus of California State University at Northridge in the heart of the sprawling San Fernando Valley. Sipping coffee and munching chocolate chip cookies as the temperature outside was beginning its relentless climb to 90 degrees, the teachers, many clad in shorts and sandals, were gathered in easy chairs that formed a lopsided circle. They listened attentively as Mark Kann, a professor at the University of Southern California, extolled the virtues of the interdisciplinary approach.

Kann advised the teachers to begin with the assumption that everything is connected. The connections, he said, should span the centuries, when appropriate. "Even the Puritans can be interesting," he said, suggesting that they be tied to today's religious sects. Kann told the teachers that an interdisciplinary approach is a more appropriate way to teach because "everything happens at once — the historical, economic, psychological, and social implications all overlap." He set the stage for the presentation that was to follow about how to prepare and teach a two-week interdisciplinary unit on slavery. The teachers were told how through a dynamic approach to the subject, cutting across the disciplines, using history, literature, art, sociology, and psychology, they could interest their students in an institution that disappeared from the country more than a century ago.

The pièce de résistance was a talk by a pair of Los Angeles high school teachers, Ray Linn and Martha Kravchek. Linn, a bearded throwback to the 1960s, whose hair was in a ponytail and who wore pink shorts, a flowery shirt, and orange sneakers, explained how the team of teachers explored the master–slave relationship to teach students about slavery. Kravchek, an English teacher, described how she used the writings of Elkins and Wright to present the slave's view of the relationship, and Linn told of how he then presented the master's view. An art teacher later showed slides of etchings of scenes of slavery that he used to enrich the lesson.

Linn launched into a discussion of Jerzy Kosinski's *Painted Bird*, his vehicle for illuminating the master–slave relationship. "You see this homeless kid getting kicked around," Linn said. "The central image in the book is very clear and good for teaching." He spoke of the bird, painted bright, unnatural colors by its sadistic keeper and sent into the sky to be attacked by other birds as symbolizing that which is different. Drawing on Sartre and Allport, Linn talked of the psychology of prejudice. "What I get into them is that human beings try to make someone different," Linn said, employing the stark street language he uses with his students to remind them of their base instincts. "I take the view in class that societies are designed to make people different." One of the teachers listening to the presentation raised the question of whether the point of view, although almost certain to appeal to students, was too one-sided in its concentration on the evil side of human nature. "We're talking of two weeks of focusing on the nasty side," said Linn. "After that it might be appropriate to give them some Buddhism."

Another teacher, Kathryn Symmes, spoke afterward of how the exposure to the interdisciplinary approach had affected her. "I always thought I was an interdisciplinary teacher because I teach literature from the standpoint of history, art, and philosophy," said Symmes. "When I teach *Huckleberry Finn*, for instance, I talk about the Civil War. What I found in working with my team members, though, was that I didn't have the expertise I thought I did and I couldn't talk about the other subjects as thoroughly as I would have wanted. I want to know when my students are reading the *Iliad* that I will be able to cross into the related disciplines with them. It will be so much richer for the students. And when our entire team is taking an interdisciplinary approach we will be able to get together as teachers and talk about strategies. We'll see others elicit responses from students and motivate them. This is making us more conscious of the way we teach," Symmes continued.

The interdisciplinary approach, which is attracting the interest of growing numbers of secondary teachers throughout the country, is a device for breaking down isolation and facilitating the sharing of knowledge among teachers. Sadie Brooks, a social studies teacher in Atlanta who participated in CHART, found that her experience enabled her to integrate more art, literature, and music into her course. In her school, Brooks said, teachers of various subjects were sufficiently motivated by the program to meet on their own before and after school to plan curriculum units together. Another Atlanta teacher, Eva Booker, who teaches art, said she saw teachers talking across disciplinary lines about substantive matters for the first time. "They are gaining a better understanding of how what each of them does in their subjects is related to what others do," Booker said. If knowledge of this sort is not empowering, then what is?

Neil Anstead, the social studies teacher who organized and directed the humanities magnet at Cleveland High School that became a model of interdisciplinary instruction for all of Los Angeles, felt that the manner in which CHART tried to introduce other teachers to the magnet spurred their intellectual growth. He said: "Teaching is entirely too private and therefore no one is there to challenge you. There are subjects that some teachers never gave much thought to before, and they are discovering they have huge blind spots. It is exciting as they design a interdisciplinary unit. It can lead to a wonderful high."

THE CONFIDENCE OF KNOWING

Dennis Lubeck in St. Louis thought this intellectual stimulus was good for teachers because usually they are divorced from content, seldom delving deeply into the material they teach nor approaching it in a scholarly manner. This detachment from scholarship has not always characterized teachers. Earlier in the century, through the 1920s and 1930s, teachers were researchers and collaborators in research with colleagues at universities (Chall, 1986). The decline in the participation in research by teachers occurred in the 1940s and 1950s, and by the 1960s and 1970s the emphasis was on university-based research, the applications of which would then be presented to teachers.

Getting teachers once again to become researchers and collaborators in research is likely to be a very slow process given the accumulated decades during which they surrendered this prerogative. But one starting point might very well be to help them recognize their profound need for intellectual growth. In sports the slogan is: "No pain; no gain." And many teachers in the Collaboratives for Humanities and Arts Teaching learned what this meant in intellectual terms. They say they were forced to come face to face with the uncomfortable reality of their own limitations. They saw this acknowledgment as a prelude to growth. Once they reconciled themselves to their deficiencies, many began taking painful strides to overcome the shortcomings that teachers often live with for a career. "Almost everyone here has taught for at least 15 years, and for the first time they are calling into question what they have done," said Ray Linn in Los Angeles. "Basically they have followed the textbook for years and let that set the tone. Now they are painfully analyzing how they teach."

Janis Nathan, a teacher with 16 years' experience in the Los Angeles public schools, who worked with fellow teachers through CHART to develop an interdisciplinary team approach to teaching, said: "I feel that I am really pushing my mind. You have a chance to open your perspective. As an English teacher it is easy to become single-minded in my discipline. Because of my experience in the program, I am now looking at everything; I look at a book from at least five separate perspectives. I didn't do that before. I am not thrilled about giving up my summer, but there is so much meat here. It works on your creative juices and that lifts your morale. The possibilities have increased for me. Ordinarily, a lot of your teaching gets repetitive without your meaning it to."

Somehow the teacher who is being asked to admit deficiencies and change has to be persuaded that there are rewards to be realized. Otherwise, why put oneself on the spot? Just setting the goal of improved teaching performance without increasing the net benefit to the one being asked to make the sacrifice may lead to frustration, low morale, defensive behavior, and unhappy consequences (Hawley, 1978). "In other words," according to Hawley, "self-awareness and high goals do not necessarily result in better teaching." Therefore, perhaps requests to change ought to be accompanied by concrete promises of empowerment — greater freedom to choose textbooks, a place on a curriculum-writing team, an assurance of being called upon to mentor a younger colleague, the promise of released time to attend seminars regularly.

The suspicion in Saint Paul was that some teachers did not assign writing because they felt obligated to mark every little mechanical mistake on the paper and therefore thought making writing assignments would be too much work for them. A goal in the writing program, sponsored by CHART was to show social studies teachers, for instance, that they could promote the writing development of their students without getting bogged down in minutiae. "That might empower them by giving them more of a sense of perspective in knowing what to expect of themselves as social studies teachers," said Carole Snyder, the school system's English supervisor.

Liz Turkes, a social studies teacher at Cleveland Junior High School in Saint Paul, was spurred by the deficiencies she felt: "I give lots of multiple-choice, true-or-false, and short-answer tests, but my favorite are essays. I want to know how to give them more often without having so much more work to do. I feel I have to put in periods and correct all the grammar with a red pen." Another Saint Paul teacher, Daniel Brick, a veteran of 17 years, believed it would make him "more powerful as a teacher" if he knew more about how to release the imaginations of his students. After his first two weekends at a CHART institute, where he learned devices for getting students to write dramatic dialogue, he was eager to learn more about how to teach writing because he found the approach so effective with his students.

Judy Brzinski, the principal of an elementary school in Saint Paul, saw her teachers become more empathetic with their students as a result of the teachers going through a clinic in which they learned to write better. "Now, they know what it feels like to be a student and to be uncomfortable and struggle," she said. "Initially, it was very threatening to them, but then they unified and became supportive of each other in the institute and that has carried over to their work in the building."

Dale Allen, a Philadelphia English teacher with a degree in English, said she never felt confident teaching writing because she was taught only about literature and not how to teach writing. "It was not until I participated in a program that gave me a systematic way of teaching writing that I was comfortable with my own writing and comfortable with teaching writing to students," Allen said. "I've had many inservice courses, but nothing ever hit me the way this thing did; it changed my method of teaching." Allen, who studied the teaching of writing in CHART, said she ceased the practice of simply assigning a topic and expecting students to write. She added a whole prewriting session in which the students map out what they will write about, drawing a circle with ideas that represent the spokes as they brainstorm their way into the assignment.

The teaching of writing aside, there are other shortcomings that some social studies teachers feel. In New York City, where CHART was a way to get teachers to examine parts of the world that they had spent much of their careers overlooking, Bob Leventhal recalled how his preparation to be a history teacher was largely devoted to learning about Europe and the United States. Now, though, under a state mandate, the schools were to do more with Asia, Africa, and Latin America. "It can be terrifying to walk into a classroom and have to teach something you've never taught before," Leventhal admitted. "As a teacher you are supposed to have insights and interpretations that go beyond simply having read the book the night before the kids did."

The areas in which most teachers feel weakest, especially at the elementary school level, are science and mathematics. A main reason so many students are shaky in science and math is because they were poorly taught the subjects in elementary school by teachers who themselves were lacking in confidence. The cycle perpetuates itself. Any strengthening of their background in these subjects is bound to give teachers a new sense of power. And that is exactly what happened to the New York City and suburban elementary school teachers who participated in the Institute for the Advancement of Mathematics and Science at Long Island University, which received funds from the National Science Foundation and the Fund for the Improvement of Postsecondary Instruction.

More than simply a college course for the teachers, the Institute was an enterprise that carried the teachers through the school year and the summer, requiring their schools to give them released time for the program. The approach very much resembled that used in CHART. Not only were the teachers taught the subject matter itself, but they delved into the methodology of presenting it to children and devised curriculum units. Because of the enthusiasm of teachers who did not want to leave the program, Madeleine J. Long, the project director, got funds for a follow-up in which 15 of the best teachers would get advanced training in math so that they could become resident math experts in their buildings. Superintendents had to promise to create new positions for these people so that they could give half their time to teaching and half to training fellow teachers.

This matter of changing one's behavior as a teacher—no small achievement for someone who has been following the same procedures for decades—cannot be underrated in its importance. Acquisition of knowledge is no guarantee that behavior will change, as attested to by the number of people who continue to drive while under the influence of alcohol despite the campaigns that have shown them the link between drunk driving and accidents. But there is certainly a better chance that once knowledge has been gained, attitudes will change and behavior will be affected.

There are countless examples in which acquiring knowledge has affected the behavior of teachers, freeing them from ways that stifled their teaching practices and empowering them to act differently. Joe Bergin, a high school English department head in Philadelphia, maintained that teachers were empowered by gaining the ability to teach writing through a process that put more of the responsibility in the hands of students. The teachers were freed of having the whole lesson center around their lecture, an ostensibly powerful role but actually one that is constraining despite its appearance of authority. "You say to yourself that if you can do this with kids—help them to teach themselves—that is *real* power," Bergin observed.

Teachers in Schenley High School in Pittsburgh gained a similar feeling about their ability to set up seminar-style discussions in which they joined the students in trying to analyze pieces of great literature. What teachers learned through the program carried out under the auspices of CHART—which encouraged the use of critical thinking seminars in all subjects, not just the humanities—were techniques that would enable them to turn over more of the responsibility for the discussion to the students. The goal so far as students were concerned was to build up their power of inquiry. As in the writing program in Philadelphia, the notion was that the teacher could grow if he or she were no longer perceived as the sole authority for all knowledge.

Yet, the teacher-centered approach is so imbedded as the main instructional model that students were slow to take the responsibility offered to them. A visitor to one class at Schenley watched the teacher struggle to draw out the students in a discussion of a portion of Schopenhauer's *The Pessimist's Handbook*. Only a minority of the class voluntarily joined the discussion, but the teacher saw the long-range potential of the approach. "When it works it gets them listening more to each other and respecting each other's ideas," the teacher, Diane Long, observed after the class. "They are better off if they don't think of teachers as the ultimate authority on everything. As strange as it may sound, I gain power by letting them see I don't have all the answers." This sort of attitude very much fits with the notion of empowerment and, in turn, with the goal of improving teaching.

Often, the kind of power teachers exercise in the classroom has to do not so much with knowledge but with setting rules for the routine to be followed by the students, not unlike the manner in which the principal prescribes the rules for the routine to which teachers are to adhere. Powell et al. (1985) write of the various "treaties" — both spoken and tacit — that exist between students and teachers. McNeil (1986) writes of "defensive teaching" in which demands on the students are reduced to make them happy and keep order, and Sarason (1982, pp. 215–33) writes of "constitutional issues." Whatever the label, the point is that too frequently the power of the teacher has been the ability to regulate the classroom bureaucracy rather than the power associated with academic knowledge and good teaching.

Sarason (pp. 220–22) suggests that the important behavior of teachers, however, is that which bears on the why's and how's of learning and thinking. He asks whether a teacher confronted by a child who does not know or cannot do something attempts to find out how the student was thinking rather than laying down the correct response for the child. Sarason asks how often the teacher says "I don't know" and proceeds to discuss how the answer might be sought. And, finally, Sarason asks how frequently and in what ways a teacher delves into the role of question asking as a tool in intellectual inquiry or problem solving.

KNOWING HOW TO CHANGE

It is sometimes forgotten among the reform movement's many calls for higher student achievement that, to an extent, changing students depends on changing teachers. Some of the ways that teachers continue to do the same old things make it unlikely that student performance will improve. The attempt in Pittsburgh to foster more dialogue in the classroom illustrates the problem. Many teachers are used to lecturing, behaving as if they were pouring information into inert vessels. "To engage students in dialogue requires change on the part of many teachers," said Richard Wallace, the Pittsburgh superintendent. He conceded that even with training not all teachers will be able to conduct discussions effectively, but said that those teachers will be empowered who can enlarge their ability to formulate questions and support discussion.

A report to the Ford Foundation on the Urban Math Collaborative (Romberg & Pitman, 1985) took note of this same problem, pointing out that for many of the teachers the transition from new ideas to application in the classroom within the traditional structure is not obvious. Nor do teachers necessarily recognize that the curriculum in its current status bodes against needed changes. "In working toward change, teachers are unsure of how to use external resources," the report stated. "For too long, materials have simply been given to teachers without giving them an opportunity to reflect, think, or argue about what needs to be done. Now, the situation has changed, but most teachers are unaware of how to ask for and use external resources." Thus, among the objectives of the Urban Math Collaborative were to get teachers to ask increasingly interesting questions of their students, to become more receptive to new ideas, to become more resourceful in their teaching, and to be more encouraging of their students' efforts to learn.

Because they generally feel that there are no rewards for stretching themselves and trying something new, teachers tend to maintain their routines and not try to make the kind of change attempted by teachers at Schenley. Teachers might be more likely to develop new materials and try fresh approaches if they could collaborate with colleagues, but in the usual school building there is not only little opportunity for such cooperation, but no particular incentive to do so. A value of a project like CHART is the incentive it provides.

The idea of such interaction with colleagues can be unsettling because it means unmasking yourself to the person in the next room and acknowledging that you might have something to learn from that person. No one likes to admit to deficiencies, especially in areas in which the person is supposed to have enough expertise to earn a living. This points to another lesson learned from CHART in some of the cities: Where it succeeded best it was nonthreatening. The knowledge was imparted in ways that didn't imply that teachers were stupid for not already knowing more than they did. This is surely a delicate matter because the fact is that in some cases the teachers, if they were conscientious, should have already had a firm handle on the material.

A problem with the usual inservice model at the school building level is that when the instruction is done by principals and assistant principals, or under their aegis, teachers worry about performance. Bosses are the last people in the world to whom teachers — or most other employees — want to confess shortcomings. The best teaching is predicated on a frank exchange in which the learner openly acknowledges what he or she doesn't know and shares his or her fears with the person doing the teaching. Otherwise the person doing the teaching has no assurance of conveying the information that the learner most needs. Thus, there is a basic problem in a system in which the person who evaluates someone is also responsible for instructing that person. For this reason, there may be little growth in the usual inservice program.

"Teachers tend to perpetuate mediocrity and shy away from creativity because they are frightened to try something new and to admit that they may not be the expert at something," said Nolan Tveter, a sixth-grade teacher in Saint Paul. Teachers may simply decide not to teach certain material with which they are uncomfortable rather than admit their deficiencies and seek help.

Teachers frequently are the victims of the inadequacy of their own education because it does not equip them to bring intellectual authority to the subject matter they teach. This failing has brought the whole approach to teacher education, as well as inservice education, into question. The problem causes some experienced teachers to worry about the academic quality of the young people who aspire to be teachers. For example, Joan Thames, a teacher at a school in Saint Paul that is a center for student teaching, said she has seen the gradual deterioration in the people entering the field. As a step toward producing brighter teachers, the Holmes Group proposed that the undergraduate major in education be scrapped so that students could first get a broad, general education and then pursue graduate professional training in the field of education. In another step, the Task Force of the Carnegie Forum recommended the creation of a national board of standards to grant certificates to qualified teachers.

In the absence of such national certification there are local requirements for licensing teachers, requirements that sometimes appear at cross-purposes with the goal of getting able teachers. In New York City, for instance, Carole Hannah Soler told of how she earned two bachelor's degrees, one in English and one in philosophy, and a master's degree in philosophy and taught in several community colleges. When she decided in 1986 that she wanted to work in the New York City public schools she took and passed the common branches examination for elementary school teachers. But she was told she would have to get another master's degree because philosophy was not a subject usually taught in elementary schools. "Six years' teaching experience, three degrees, and honor awards seem not yet to qualify me to teach first grade," Soler said (1987). Most highly rated private schools would welcome a candidate with such credentials.

Whatever the ultimate changes in licensing procedures and teacher education, greater empowerment will be produced only if teachers get the knowledge that enables them to take on more intellectual responsibility. Until now, teachers have often let others make decisions for them, not only because teachers did not have the authority but also because teachers did not have some of the knowledge they needed to reach an informed decision. Sometimes only an outsider notices how much teachers take it for granted that curricula will be developed for them by others, as though they are not qualified to be involved in deciding what they will teach and in doing the research to create the units. Teachers are so used to the absence of power that they may not realize it is missing. Michael Grigsby, who gave up a career as an oceanographer with a federal agency to become a schoolteacher in Seattle, said he was "appalled to learn that it wasn't classroom teachers who developed the curriculum."

Gregory Anrig, president of the Educational Testing Service, maintained that the teacher must have a central role in determining curriculum content "for effective teaching and learning to take place" (1987). He proposed that the role of teachers extend into selection of textbooks and standardized tests. Yet, most teachers do not have that role. Reforms fail because the teacher is cast in the "role of user rather than creator of curriculum ideas and materials" (Common, 1983). The ensuing power struggle between the reformers who would impose top-down change on teachers rather than letting it come up from the teachers ends up producing no change at all, according to Common. Teachers, in effect, have veto power in instances where they do not have the power to implement. This kind of power is basically negative. Were teachers truly empowered and accorded a key role in determining curriculum, then substantial change might result.

TEACHERS TEACHING TEACHERS

Certainly one way in which the education of new teachers can be augmented in a manner that empowers veteran teachers is to turn over some of the responsibility for educating colleagues to the best of the experienced teachers, as was sometimes done in the Rockefeller and Ford programs. This is what the proposals for career ladders usually include, and the approach has the advantage of being acceptable to teachers' unions because it awards extra pay for added work, rather than the merit pay concept that is anathema to unions. One example of what is possible is the pilot program in New York City, where 45 experienced teachers served as mentors to 90 new teachers. Using money allocated by the state, the school system hired enough teachers to release the participating teachers from a portion of their work load. The mentors had 10 percent of their time available to meet with and observe the interns. The interns had 20 percent of their time available to meet with the mentors, observe experienced teachers, attend workshops, and prepare materials.

On a national basis there is the Teachers Teaching Teachers program of the Woodrow Wilson National Fellowship Foundation. This venture, for high school math and science teachers, brings teachers to Princeton University for four weeks of training during the summer, and those who have been through the program themselves become presenters to other teachers during the school year. "The unforeseen degree of success of the program is due to the fact that high school teachers not only trust their peers, but are proud of them and respond enthusiastically to their teaching," according to the Woodrow Wilson Foundation (1986).

What is most important here from the standpoint of empowerment is that veteran teachers take on a portion of one of the most vital functions in the school: the continuing professional education of fellow teachers. And they don't have to give up teaching and become administrators to do it. The imprint that the mentors place on the novices will affect the teaching of the new people for years to come.

Schenley High School in Pittsburgh, which doubles as a teaching center, is a leading example of a venture in which teachers train each other. Several dozen teachers from throughout the district are released from their own schools, eight weeks at a time, to report to Schenley, which is an operating high school for 1,000 students. The resident, handpicked faculty members at Schenley do regular teaching and work with the visiting teachers—developing and teaching seminars, serving as role models, and participating in clinical programs to "coach" the visitors. Each resident teacher is assigned two visiting teachers, who carry out teaching assignments with classes at Schenley under the tutelage of the resident teacher. Meanwhile, back in the visiting teacher's home school, his or her classes are being taught by teachers who completed the training at Schenley and are engaged in follow-up activities.

The structure of schoolteaching, which in most districts until now has not involved teachers formally working with each other to perfect their craft, is surely one of the barriers to empowerment. Schenley is one model for overcoming the obstacles of the past. There are other possibilities. Elementary and secondary teachers could probably gain from projects similar to the experiment at Indiana University, where ten professors, none of them physical scientists, sat in for three weeks as "students" in a physics class taught by a colleague. They not only learned something about a subject with which none were terribly familiar, but they also get extended exposure to someone else's style of teaching and were able to make suggestions — from the vantage of a learner — on how the teaching could be improved. It was part of a project, known as Peer Perspectives on Science, that its originator, Sheila Tobias of the University of Arizona, planned to carry out with foundation support at several universities around the country.

If the structure of schools allowed teachers to work more with colleagues and watch each other teach more frequently, they might well exert their power in ways that would reduce incompetence on the staff. Ideally, this exercise of authority would extend beyond methodology and into more of the decisions affecting the curriculum itself so that teachers would have the opportunity to register opinions and have those views considered as policy is shaped. In one of the cities in CHART there was the striking example of a reading program — unrelated to CHART — that teachers were ordered to implement, never having been consulted about the program or given a chance to voice their reservations. They effectively sabotaged it because they did not believe in it, and the whole venture turned into a mess.

Teachers who have a role in determining what they will teach feel a sense of ownership that is likely to be beneficial to their teaching. On the other hand, their teaching may suffer if they do not feel at one with the material they are required to present. "A lot of new curriculum gets written by just a few people, and then the others don't buy into it," said Bill Hampton, the former principal in the St. Louis area. When their own learning is directed toward curriculum development, there is a connection that makes it more exciting and probably enhances the ability of teachers to use the material. Sheila H. Smith, an instructional specialist in Los Angeles, saw an advantage in the interdisciplinary curriculum developed through CHART: "We are not giving them a curriculum; they are designing their own." An emphasis in Ford's Urban Mathematics Collaborative Project was the idea that teachers were not being given anything other than the knowledge and opportunity to work individually and in groups to fashion units and materials that they thought would help them teach math better. This was a refreshing change from the old inservice model of delivering enlightenment to the naked natives.

There is, however, a downside to all this, a question of just how much of the curriculum development can be left to the teachers, even if time is made available and they are paid for the work. It is a question of qualifications. Can "instant experts" really plan a proper curriculum? Many teachers essentially are novices in the areas in which they are delving. Certainly this is not true of all teachers, some of whom have long been given school-wide or district-wide responsibility for planning. The problem is that too many others, the majority, have never been involved in writing a new curriculum from scratch and they have not kept close enough to the scholarship in their fields to make the contributions that are needed.

On the other hand, empowering teachers to take more authority for the curriculum has to start someplace. It is certainly one of the areas in which teachers must get more deeply involved if empowerment is to take on meaning. After all, teachers must have more to say about what is being taught if they are going to be taken seriously as professionals. This is an area in which college professors and other subject experts might be able to provide their greatest service to schoolteachers. There is nothing about empowerment that precludes consultation with authorities. It certainly appears worth the risk to give teachers more control over curriculum development. But the product ought to be carefully monitored.

Beyond their need for knowledge that will enhance their qualifications, teachers sorely need knowledge that is presented in a way that motivates them. Even when the material itself has been worthwhile there frequently has been little impact on the performance of teachers in the classroom. Giving a teacher new information, however interesting and useful, is not enough in itself to change old habits. Teachers have often been as impervious to what was taught to them in inservice as were the students to whom they directed lessons in their classrooms. Students, it seems, are not the only ones in schools who are unmotivated. Burnout has taken a toll among teachers and is a main reason why teaching is sometimes so uninspiring and why some teachers do nothing to make themselves more informed on the topics they teach.

While an enterprise like CHART seemed to motivate teachers it may be not so much that the Rockefeller Foundation had found a panacea as that it also had a lot of money. First of all, the teachers were paid for much of their participation. There was also the Rockefeller name to open doors, getting those administrators who were recalcitrant to cooperate and encouraging prestigious clubs and societies to let their facilities be used for meetings. A big question is the extent to which similar programs—without as ample funding and without the prestige and influence—can generate the same zealousness for learning among teachers. There certainly are principles to be gleaned from CHART that have broad application. The teachers seemed to be making an important point when they said of CHART that it was not that they were paid, but how they were treated that counted. This should never be forgotten in inservice education of any kind.

REACHING STUDENTS

Finally, unless such programs ultimately promote the learning of students, the experience of the teachers—however rewarding—does not really improve education. It is fine to make teachers smarter and more excited about their work, but the benefits must be transmitted to students if the program is to be worthwhile. What it comes down to, according to Sizer (1984), is that the function of the teacher—the reason schools exist—is to assist the student to learn. And it is not easy to translate new knowledge and zeal into a form that will benefit the students, especially those who resist.

This means that what has been taught to the teacher must, first, be put into a form that is understandable, interesting, and perhaps even entertaining for the students to whom the teacher will present it. Second, and very much related, it must be presented in a manner and in a setting that motivates students to want to learn it. In William Glasser's control theory there is the assertion that people struggle to gain control over their lives by satisfying basic needs, one of them being the need for power (Gough, 1987). To students this means being able to believe that someone is listening to them and acknowledging their importance. Students, particularly those for whom getting into college and conforming are not very important, will not work if they do not feel their needs are taken seriously by the teacher.

Where both CHART and the Urban Math Collaborative worked best, teachers came away with the ability and insight to use their knowledge in the classroom. "Many seminars in the past gave us knowledge, but we did not learn how to disseminate it," said Jeffrey Cabat, social studies chairman at Seward Park High School in New York City. "This time they gave us direct applicability to the classroom and that is power." Teachers in some cities told of how they would not let a college professor finish a seminar without first stopping to discuss how the material could be adapted to their students. This should become a guiding principle in inservice education.

Nonetheless, motivating students to want to learn the new material can be difficult. "We finally have discovered what we want to teach, but no one has discovered the ways of doing it," said Alonzo Crim, the superintendent in Atlanta. "There are young people who say, 'School is not my top priority.' Not all of them want to be educated. That's what we're struggling with."

Teachers, the ones who must confront this reality firsthand, are very much engaged in the struggle to which Crim alluded. "How do I take it to a gang member who has no desire for the knowledge?" asked Richard Y. Takagaki, a social studies teacher in Los Angeles, who had widened his own knowledge through CHART. "How do you turn them on? There are certain assumptions in this program about the students and their willingness to learn." Intuition tells one that teachers who are better informed and more dedicated to their calling will more readily reach the students. But some teachers question this notion and are not so sure that students will want to learn just because the teacher is enthusiastic and well prepared and the material is properly conceived.

Just how far can even the best teacher go in an era when the social pathology that envelops the lives of so many young people seems an impenetrable obstacle to education? The syndrome of poverty, malnutrition, early pregnancy, drugs, and lack of reinforcement for schooling in the home can cut the legs out from under even the most dedicated teacher. More than one-third of all Hispanic children and more than 40 percent of all black children reside in poverty. In urban school systems, where Rockefeller and Ford placed their emphases, as many as half the students do not remain in school long enough to graduate. At least one-quarter of the girls who drop out are pregnant or already have babies. The number of households headed by teenage mothers who dropped out of school is growing rapidly. The sense of lack of control such young people feel, whether they remain in school or drop out, is enormous, and if one subscribes to the Glasser theory, this is a fundamental barrier to their motivation.

Yet, in its own paradoxical way the empowerment of teachers remains linked to the empowerment of students. The sort of power most important for more knowledgeable teachers to exert is that which enhances the learning and development of children in their classrooms. Cummins (1986) holds that it is up to educators to redefine their role vis-à-vis minority students — more readily teaching to the students' strengths and not orienting themselves toward deficits — if those young people are to become effective learners. Similarly, Burbules (1986) maintains that teachers must feel sufficiently empowered to be innovative and autonomous in their teaching style, if to do so is in the best interests of their students. But for teachers to have the impact they would like to have on students there will have to be some societal changes as well as some structural changes in schools that make young people more desirous of learning. Teachers in an urban setting and, to a lesser degree, teachers elsewhere must therefore build into their pursuit of power the effort to empower students so that they will want to learn.

4 ▹▸

PARTNERS IN EDUCATION

TWO SECTORS outside the public schools can play a special role in the empowerment of teachers: higher education and business. Practitioners in both have more prestige than schoolteachers have, and, moreover, specialized knowledge is the bedrock upon which those sectors are built. There is much that higher education and business can provide to teachers if the proper connections are made. Advances toward empowerment are likely to be abetted by those ties. All three of the foundation programs described in this book—those of Rockefeller, Ford, and Carnegie—relied greatly on the involvement of universities and businesses.

Collaboration by schoolteachers with colleagues who work outside the schools can help teachers widen their vision and feel a part of a larger enterprise. If teachers think of themselves as having such connections and if, eventually, they are perceived by others as being tied into a collegial network that extends into higher education and business, then surely this will be a boost toward empowerment.

It is also important in this context to note the role that foundations generally, both local and national, can assume in aiding teachers by providing financial support for enterprises such as CHART and similar projects. What Rockefeller was seeking to trigger with its contribution in each city was a community-wide collaboration with other funders. In St. Louis, for instance, the International Education Consortium also got money from the Danforth and McDonnell Foundations. In Saint Paul, the Dialogue program of Compas also got backing from the Saint Paul Foundation, the National Endowment for the Arts, and the Matsushita Foundation. Other partners in the collaborations were corporations, public agencies, and the school systems themselves, which pledged specific amounts of financial support.

HIGHER EDUCATION

The structure of the teaching profession in higher education is not a paradigm for elementary and secondary education, but the Collaboratives for Humanities and Arts Teaching was just one more way of confirming that all of education could gain by closer associations between the two sectors. "We're doing the same job; we're just seeing learners at different points along the continuum," said Marie Collins, a Los Angeles teacher. "Without an exchange neither of us will know what the other is doing. They can make us feel valued."

The fact is that more prestige is attached to higher education than to elementary and secondary schools. That in itself is a reason for building linkages. But it is more complex than that. Ties between schools and colleges have the potential of helping schoolteachers improve their craft. The most obvious contribution to the teachers is the knowledge they can get from professors who have more time to become experts in their subjects. But colleges also can facilitate contacts among teachers, provide settings for teachers to hone their skills, and give teachers entrée to research facilities and other amenities that add to their professionalization.

For many years, the two sectors went their separate ways. Once schoolteachers finished their formal education they seldom had dealings with higher education, and the lack of contact led each side to regard the other with suspicion. Stereotypes abound in the minds of educators from each side in thinking about the other. Relations seldom have been good between teachers and professors. "Often, university people are contemptuous of school people," said Judith Hodgson in Philadelphia, who before leading PATHS was a university teacher and administrator. "They think school people are not bright enough to be professors. We hammer away at this attitude without making headway." Writer Paul Woodring (1987) argued that the demise of the Master of Arts in Teaching programs that were established at a number of prestigious liberal arts colleges in the 1960s was largely because of hostile attitudes by professors in the rest of the college toward teacher education and the kinds of students who seek employment in the public schools.

Until the situation began to improve in the mid-1980s, it could largely be described this way: "Institutions of higher education have remained aloof. Aside from the obvious role of preparing the men and women who teach in elementary and secondary schools, colleges and universities have been reluctant to enter into partnerships designed to enhance cooperation between the two sectors. In many cases, high schools have been left without any sense of what the colleges expect graduates to know" (Maeroff, 1983, p. 1).

On the other hand, schoolteachers, thinking about professors, have considered them narrow-gauged, supercilious people out of touch with the real world, the realm in which schoolteachers work. Schoolteachers often regard professors as poor teachers who have never developed their pedagogical skills to anywhere near the level possessed by the schoolteachers. A mathematics teacher at Lawless High School in New Orleans said he was not enthusiastic about the Urban Math Collaborative because of what he detected as a built-in assumption that secondary school teachers necessarily have something to learn from college math professors. He said his skills were already on a very advanced level.

Contributing to the division between the sectors are the differences in training and in the ways that schoolteachers and university professors go about their work. "The schoolteacher's job description, then, is one that none of our universities would ever visit on a member of their faculties," the Holmes Group (1986, p. 7) reminded readers of its report. "For they know that teachers who work under such conditions have no time left to learn themselves, to be productive scholars, or even to do justice to their students' homework."

Experience has shown, however, that despite differences in the nature of their work, rapprochement is possible if the right kinds of bridges are set in place. Part of the improvement comes just from getting schoolteachers and professors talking to each other. "The university people we see get to better understand the public school teachers," said Roger Kurtz, a schoolteacher in a district near St. Louis.

Two Different Worlds

Dee Pinkerton, who in his three decades of teaching in Seattle was never involved with a university professor as a colleague until 1985 when he was part of a team writing a unit for teaching economics to ninth graders, summed up the relationship this way: "This was my first time having a university professor as a professional colleague on an institutional basis. They were colleagues, not dictating to us. It is good for them and really terrific for us. It adds to your prestige to associate with them and gives you the feeling you know something about the subject because you can discuss it with them." Bill Peacock, a veteran teacher in Atlanta, found that the first opportunity for better relations came at the beginning of CHART when the professor who was leading a session "just introduced himself by name instead of having a lot of airs and saying 'I am Doctor So and So, Professor of Such and Such.'"

A basic difference in the tasks facing schoolteachers and professors has to do with their students. Professors have a voluntary audience, and schoolteachers have a captive audience. Schoolteachers must be much more adept at the skills of teaching to hold the attention of their students. Kathryn Symmes, a Los Angeles teacher, saw in CHART how the relationships between teachers and professors evolved as recognition of this difference sank in: "At first the university people just offered us a description of how they did things. Then there would be some interaction in the halls afterward and we would tell them about the reality of how we do things. Then they would start thinking more and more about the demands on us and how they could get down in the trenches with us. They would say, 'You have the tougher job. I couldn't imagine teaching *The Scarlet Letter* to those kinds of kids. And, besides, you have to see so many of them in class every day.' The result of this interaction between us and the university people is that there has been a great deal of sharing of feelings and ideas."

Some professors strive to take the special needs of schoolteachers into consideration when presenting knowledge to them. In Atlanta, for example, when Harry Rusche of Emory University was lecturing on Shakespeare to secondary school teachers in CHART, he continually offered suggestions for involving the students. "Let them design sets and costumes and write program notes," he said. "It will get them into the background of the period and they will learn more than they expect to learn." He agonized with the teachers over the problem that Elizabethan English presents in turning off teenagers. He urged the teachers to help the students get familiar with the characters before reading the play and recommended that rather than starting at the beginning of a work like *Macbeth* they might be more likely to capture the interest of students by beginning the play with the knocking at the gate of hell. "I wouldn't worry about reading the whole play," Rusche said. "Take individual scenes and work them through."

The extent to which there is room for embellishing contacts between teachers and professors can be seen at a level as fundamental as the subject area in which people teach. Seldom do teachers in high school and professors in college explore their common disciplinary concerns even though one group has as its students those who were groomed by the other group. Assuredly there must be common ground among those who teach in the same discipline whatever the level on which they teach.

Yet, such joint explorations are unusual. Allan Scholl, an administrator in Los Angeles, has seen the difficulty of trying to encourage such contacts. "I've tried to get history professors to adopt schools, but it's difficult to get them to do this," Scholl said. "I'd love to see university people accept high school teachers as colleagues. In Europe, university people traditionally start teaching at secondary schools and then go on to university teaching. Here, there is a tremendous chasm between the two, and the only experience that most university professors have with high school is that they once attended one."

The problem has to do with "downward coupling." In Europe, secondary education is tightly coupled to the university, but in the United States, where elementary and secondary schools are grouped together within school districts, the coupling of secondary education tends mostly to be with elementary education (Clark, 1985). This downward coupling underscores the differences, rather than the commonalities, in the mission of college professors and high school teachers. Thus, it becomes more difficult to forge the sort of ties between them that might be helpful.

Bridging the Gap

Among the contributions of the recent impetus for closer cooperation between schools and colleges are the formal groups created to bring together those from the secondary and higher education levels who teach the same subject. A leader in this trend was Claire Gaudiani of the University of Pennsylvania, who got several foundations to back her effort to form the first of these collaborations in the various fields of the humanities. Proceeding on the premise that "adults who teach the same subject in the same geographic area share a collective responsibility for the quality of each other's teaching and learning," she brought together teachers from the schools and from higher education (Gaudiani & Burnett, 1986). Her idea of alliances has been widely replicated; the *Chronicle of Higher Education* (1987) reported that there were 15 such groups in English in 11 states, 105 groups in foreign languages in 37 states, 7 groups in geography in 6 states, and 35 groups in history in 18 states. The trend has spread beyond the humanities, according to the *Chronicle* survey, which found 50 groups of teachers and professors devoted to mathematics in 30 states.

Participating in such alliances can be an empowering experience for teachers. Obviously, there are no guarantees about how effective the alliances will be, but where the effort succeeds teachers can take a large stride toward breaking out of their isolation and digging into their fields in ways that, besides helping them in the classroom, will make them feel much better about themselves. Teachers do not have the time that professors do to keep abreast of research, but the chance to discuss scholarship is a new experience for many teachers. "The whole point of collaboration is to help teachers rediscover the reasons why they went into teaching—collegiality, love of ideas, reaching into young minds, esteem of the profession, personal intellectual growth," said Ben Ladner, director of the National Faculty, an organization based in Atlanta that has a roster of hundreds of professors whom it sends into schools to work with teachers. The National Faculty provided the professors who were consultants to teachers in Atlanta for CHART.

For their part, professors, too, can gain from alliances, though usually not to the same degree as teachers since they have built into their jobs more opportunities for interaction with colleagues in their discipline. But in an era in which remedial education is so widespread, it may be that by having closer ties to the teachers who deal with students before they get to college, professors will better understand the reasons for the need for remediation once students are in college. Anyone familiar with education on both levels knows well that there is a great deal of common ground shared by teachers and professors who are having trouble teaching students to write, handle mathematics, and think critically. Many professors could also benefit from discussions with schoolteachers about teaching methodology.

One way to encourage collaboration between teachers and professors is to mandate it. The History Teachers Institute, sponsored throughout the state by the New York Council for the Humanities in the summer of 1984, required that scholars who wanted to direct programs had to develop their proposals in consultation with high school teachers. The fallout from such collaboration was such that one consortium of college and high school people, whose proposal was not funded, had generated so much enthusiasm and good feeling that the members organized the project on their own.

The more teachers and professors are put in contact, the more they are likely to learn about each other. The main problem is that there is a paucity of mechanisms for facilitating this contact. The need for greater mutual understanding is profound. Even little differences between teachers and professors sometimes go unrecognized. When Washington University in St. Louis decided to invite high school teachers to join professors at an art exhibit on campus in connection with CHART, the setting for their contact was a wine-and-cheese reception at which people stood around making small talk. It wasn't until afterward that the well-intentioned folks at the university realized that, unlike the professors, the teachers had spent the entire day on their feet and their idea of relaxing was to be able to sit down, not to continue standing. Had the university people been cognizant of that little difference between the way that teachers and professors go about their craft, the event might have involved having everyone sit down.

From his perspective on the other side of the Great Divide, Michael Gomez, a professor at Washington University, found so much enthusiasm among the teachers he taught in the summer institute of CHART that some of them joined him on a trip to Senegal. "I have had a rewarding time working with the teachers," he said. "They appreciate it because it is an opportunity for them to explore issues that they wouldn't otherwise be teaching about. The teachers appear to enjoy the interaction and seem to be learning a lot. They are picking up what they should have gotten in their formal training. My role is mostly tutorial because the teachers don't know a lot about Africa. Some teachers got so interested that they plan to attend the African studies meeting this year."

Some people at Washington University worked assiduously to understand schoolteachers, and, in turn, many of the teachers also tried to erase their own stereotypes and open themselves to new attitudes toward the professors. Linda Salamon, the dean at the university, said she saw genuine growth among the participants in the Collaboratives for Humanities and Arts Teaching. "There was a timidity in their thinking at the outset, a defensiveness; they expected the professors would talk down to them and that they would have to keep proving themselves to the professors and to each other," Salamon said of the teachers. "By the third summer, they felt like the professors were colleagues of theirs, and they felt comfortable."

One professor, Joel Glassman of the University of Missouri at St. Louis, who was involved with schoolteachers through CHART agreed that the program seemed to be a boon to the teachers. Glassman pointed to the benefits: "What we're doing is broadening the horizons of teachers. They appreciate the opportunity to interact at an intellectual level. They are finally in an atmosphere where they can talk to someone and there is a genuine exchange of ideas and information. It is different from the normal course they might take as part of continuing education at a college. The teachers are very enthusiastic. There has been personal growth for them and it's valuable for me because I'm teaching better, more motivated students than the average undergraduate."

Glassman said the Asian studies group in St. Louis, made up essentially of college professors, developed an outreach program for high school teachers, a small number of whom he said reached a high level of professional competence in China or Japan. In addition, there were such contributions as a Sinologist reviewing textbooks with teachers to try to ensure an accurate portrayal of Maoism. There was potential for much more of this sort of cooperation since Washington University published a directory of college professors willing to work with high school teachers.

At one time the main relationship that schoolteachers had with institutions of higher education was through the colleges of education. This is less and less the case. As Washington University, Yale University, and other institutions have demonstrated, the arts and sciences provide fertile ground for planting seeds of cooperation. Oberlin College in Ohio, for instance, which has no education school, is operating its Oberlin College Teachers Institute to help Cleveland public school teachers in the content areas. Summer programs, including those that take teachers abroad for study, workshops throughout the schoolyear, and other features, fortify the academic background of teachers and increase their confidence. Oberlin, which got foundation funding for the institute, admitted there was some "self-interest" in the hope that the college's involvement would also lead the teachers to talk to some of their brightest graduating seniors about attending Oberlin.

Another higher education institution in the Cleveland area, John Carroll University, stepped up its involvement with the schools through its mathematics department. The university, in conjunction with the Cleveland Collaborative for Mathematics Education, sponsors an Algebra Contest for high schools, in which about forty teams of four students competed in the spring of 1987. The idea for the contest, which is to be an annual event, arose after members of the university faculty felt that incoming students lacked adequate preparation in algebra. During the year a professor from John Carroll visits high schools and holds workshops with students on the questions used in the previous year's contest.

Yet, as welcome as the involvement of higher education might be, the question is how much can colleges really do for teachers in helping them toward empowerment. "The teachers are better educated and learning what they should have learned in college and I see positive growth," said Professor Glassman in St. Louis. "They don't feel they do that through their jobs, which are not ordinarily learning experiences. For university professors, learning is built into the job. Schoolteachers have to get it on the side. The problem is the structure of their employment; it isn't a problem of aloofness by the universities. They teach six hours a day, and they don't even have their own offices. There is no time to develop expertise."

There is, too, the issue of how far collaboration with higher education can go without the deep commitment of the academy. Professors are promoted and awarded tenure primarily on the basis of scholarship. Young professors still trying to ascend the academic hierarchy could jeopardize their status by devoting time to an activity—working with schoolteachers—for which there is little recognition in their reward structure. Therefore the success of cooperation often depends on the participation of tenured professors, who do not have to worry so much about making points with their academic departments.

One wonders just how many veteran members of the professoriate will care to get involved with elementary and secondary schools, an unglamorous enterprise compared with consulting or writing a book. But there are signs of a changing attitude among professors, and finally there is some very real potential for collaboration of the kind that might help lift the status of schoolteachers closer to that of college professors. If the professoriate helps bring that about, it will have made a huge contribution to the teachers. One favorable sign is the recommendation by a commission in California that faculty members at the state's publicly supported universities get credit toward promotion and tenure for services performed in behalf of public school systems.

BUSINESS

In much the same vein as the relations with higher education, contacts between schools and business were sporadic at best and often nonexistent. Only since the early 1980s, when the Adopt-a-School idea began to spread, has there been a change. Many of the advantages that accrue to teachers in dealing with professors are also available in closer contacts with business. Hodgson observed: "One thing that bringing them together has done is show businesspeople that schoolteachers aren't people who sit around doing nothing. Until they talk to the teachers, the businesspeople don't know just how bad it is in some schools, places where teachers are trying to teach reading to kids who are nearly inarticulate because adults haven't really spoken with them—kids who are hungry because they haven't eaten breakfast and have bruises and contusions because they are abused. Businesspeople learn about this."

One businessperson who said that being put in contact with schools and teachers was an eye-opener is John Steinbrunner, an actuary with Wyatt Company who was active in the Cleveland Collaborative for Mathematics Education. He said: "I wasn't aware of the extent of the problems. It is inconceivable to me that a teacher would like to use a certain math textbook and the principal won't approve it. It hit home when I discovered some of the obstacles that teachers face on a day-to-day basis. I've come out of these meetings with no doubt that teachers are underpaid. I didn't see that before."

Corporations ranging from Rich's Department Store in Atlanta to Hewlett-Packard, the high-technology company in California's Silicon Valley, have gotten involved in dropout prevention programs. Others are working with individual schools, such as Westinghouse is doing in Pittsburgh with the school system's high school of science. Some businesses that once matched only the gifts that employees made to institutions of higher education are now matching gifts to elementary and secondary schools. The State of Georgia ran an advertisement in the *Wall Street Journal* in 1987, aimed of course at businesspeople, boasting that it was good business for the state to be spending more than half its budget on education. Individual companies and groups of companies, such as those that banded together under the flag of the Boston Compact, have promised college scholarships and jobs after graduation to elementary and secondary students to motivate them and keep them from dropping out.

Finding Common Interests

The big question in all this is what schools and business have to gain from each other. So far as business is concerned, there is the broad objective of making a community a better place in which to turn a profit. Business needs employees, consumers, and a supportive—or at least nonhostile—environment. Business can suffer when students drop out of schools or graduate without the skills and attitudes that will make them productive in the workplace. High school graduates who are ill-equipped for entry-level jobs must be trained by the companies that hire them. Business, as a major contributor to the tax rolls, must bear part of the burden when those who have gone through the public schools end up incapable of pursuing a livelihood and receive public assistance. When the general public is not understanding of business and sympathizes with increased regulation and higher taxes, the cost of doing business rises. And, finally, an undesirable school system may make it more difficult for business to attract talented employees from other locales. Thus, business has some very practical reasons for helping the public schools.

When spokespeople from business joined officials of the National Assessment of Educational Progress in releasing a report on literacy, the people from business stressed that the need for literacy was as much their concern as that of the educators. Statements were made about the entry-level skills of workers being below what is needed for a fiercely competitive global economy. Moreover, alluding to the lower level of literacy that the National Assessment found among black and Hispanic students, the business representatives pointed out that such deficiencies meant that corporations would have to take on more and more of the training that should have been done by schools as the portion of minority students in the enrollment grew.

In speaking to other executives about getting involved in helping the public schools, William S. Woodside, chairman of Primerica Corporation, formerly American Can Company, said he concentrated on "the loss of an effective labor force. As business gets more and more complicated, we're producing students who can do fewer and fewer complicated things. . . . The other thing I talk about is that education is one of the first steps toward making an adequate income. If you're surrounded by a world where most of the incomes are inadequate how do you expect to survive as a corporation and sell your products?" (1986).

In addition to the motivation of self-interest, which, after all, should not be surprising since a corporation exists to make profits, altruism is sometimes involved in the efforts of business to aid the public schools. The hearts and souls of businesspeople, no less than those of others, are sensitive to the needs of their communities, and some credit must be given to business for wanting to help the public schools simply out of a desire for good corporate citizenship. "Our company has a commitment to precollege math and science, and we were looking for a productive way to improve urban education in those subjects," said Sondra Hardis of Standard Oil Company, which joined the Cleveland Collaborative for Mathematics Education. For years, Hardis said, her company had not gotten involved with the city's schools for lack of confidence in the school district's administrative leadership.

What is most intriguing are the many forms that corporate involvement in the schools can take. At the outset, some educators thought it best if business dumped money on the schools and kept its distance. They seemed to expect corporate limousines to roar up, drop off bundles of money at the schoolhouse door, and depart, leaving businesses with no further connection with the schools. Of course, business executives never saw it that way.

Financial donations assuredly have figured in the school–business connection, but they have not been the major element and often cash donations have not been involved at all. Business has more than money to give the schools and, for the most part, sees its role in the public schools as being something other than playing Sugar Daddy. This, though, is not to say that corporate donations are unimportant; more than 10 percent of the revenues for CHART in the various cities in the 1986–87 school year came from corporations, which also provided non-cash support. It was the hope of both Rockefeller and Ford in their ventures with the schools to get funds for the programs from the corporate sector, as well as to enlist business executives in the leadership of the projects. Rockefeller's Alberta Arthurs saw the financial commitment of corporations as one of the most favorable omens for the public schools. These are the main forms of business involvement in the schools.

> *Donating Money and Equipment.* Cash contributions to public schools by business have not materialized to the degree that some educators expected, and more frequently business has given both new and used equipment, computers being a leading example. Sometimes the donations have taken the form of college scholarships promised to the graduates of inner city high schools.
>
> *Giving Advice and Guidance.* School systems and individual schools have gotten advice from business on such matters as fiscal and personnel procedures, and some other forms of expertise have been provided as needed.
>
> *Lending Employees.* Both teaching and administrative employees have been lent to schools — usually for a semester or a year at a time — by business, though this practice is far more prevalent in higher education than it is in elementary and secondary education.
>
> *Making Jobs Available.* Summer jobs for both students and teachers are among the most promising contributions that business can provide.
>
> *Helping with Inservice Education.* Business has been drawn into some of the programs sponsored by outside agencies involved in providing inservice education for teachers.
>
> *Providing Facilities and Prestige.* It takes little effort on the part of business to let teachers and students use corporate facilities for meetings and ceremonies, but such settings often allow the kind of change of pace that goes far toward raising morale. Recognition awards by business also confer extra status on students and teachers.
>
> *Opening Lines of Contact.* One dividend of the contacts that some educators have established with businesspeople is the assistance that has been given in opening doors to government officials, foundation officers, and other business executives.
>
> *Supporting Campaigns to Win Fiscal Elections and to Lobby Legislative Bodies in Making Allocations.* A prime example of this was the statement at a Congressional hearing in 1987 by business leaders calling for increased federal funding for the Chapter 1 program for disadvantaged pupils.

The implications for the empowerment of teachers are as varied as these many avenues of business involvement in the public schools. Some of the connections have little to offer teachers per se, but other kinds of ties cannot help but add to empowerment, as teachers in some cities are discovering. Each corporation seems to fashion its own approach, sometimes seeming to strain for uniqueness. Pizza Hut tried to motivate students in elementary schools to read more books in their spare time by giving them certificates for free pizzas. Metropolitan Life gave cash prizes to schools with exemplary programs to encourage better personal health habits among students. Burger King supported an annual symposium to bring together outstanding teachers and high school principals for discussions of professional practices. Chevron produced films and other materials — most of which had nothing to do with oil — to distribute free to the schools.

A particularly intriguing project was that of Primerica Corporation in Bedford County, Tennessee, where the company provided the bulk of the funds to enable local community service agencies to hire teachers for summer jobs (Hoffman, 1987). The money not only assured the teachers of a supplement to their teaching salaries, but also produced a fruitful exchange of contacts and ideas between the teachers and the regular agency employees. A problem was that there was not enough money to hire more than two dozen teachers a year. Moreover, Primerica sold its plant to another company, leaving further corporate participation in question.

One of the most obvious ways that business can help school systems is simply by teaching them how to run their noninstructional activities in ways that private enterprise operates. In Philadelphia, business executives quickly recognized that they could make major contributions by providing advice in such areas as transportation, real estate, health care, fringe benefit programs, and personnel. Business leaders even aided the school system in its search for a high-ranking personnel officer. The businesspeople also provided a sounding board to the superintendent as she devised the fiscal plan needed to implement the school system's educational objectives. "We helped them focus on better use of resources and to examine what kind of revenues they needed," said Ralph Saul, a key business leader.

What Teachers Can Gain

For teachers, some of the links to business and industry lend a bit of status and prestige that may rub off. "When a corporate executive talks to you as an equal and asks your opinion, it makes you feel very important," said Bob Leventhal, a New York City teacher. There is a taste of this each time teachers use corporate facilities for their meetings. Teachers are also enhanced by the ties they build with corporate counterparts, as, for example, mathematics teachers in Los Angeles found through the Ford Foundation's Urban Mathematics Collaborative Project. Teachers said it was uplifting to talk about mathematics with mathematicians in business and industry. Teachers also have gotten part-time corporate jobs that added to their pay, letting them gain new knowledge and enhancing their status.

The exposure to business helps keep teachers in touch with the working world and the demands that will be made on their students by employers. Surely a teacher who has an understanding of what a young person will be asked to do in the workplace can better help a student prepare for employment. Too many teachers do not have this kind of up-to-date knowledge. When a group of Cleveland teachers visited a robotics training facility, they said they realized just how much more they had to do to get their students ready for jobs. One avenue open to Cleveland teachers who want to get firsthand experience in the workplace is the Cleveland Teacher Internship Program, an activity that attracted few teachers from the Cleveland public schools until the arrival of the Cleveland Collaborative for Mathematics Education, which cultivated new internships and encouraged the formerly demoralized mathematics teachers from the city school system to apply.

If business can become a rung on the career ladder for top teachers, it will mean both increased income and prestige for those teachers. It will also be a way for teachers to keep abreast of their fields. This can be a special opportunity for teachers of science and mathematics, letting them go in and out of industry and thereby helping to keep them from leaving teaching altogether. Internships in a corporate position during the summer or sabbaticals can end up promoting the empowerment of teachers. A teacher who returns to the classroom after time spent with IBM, the local phone company, or a regional manufacturer will look at his or her teaching job differently, and there is a good chance that the administration will regard that teacher in a new light.

Gerald G. Gold of the National Institute for Work and Learning cited six principal benefits to teachers who participate in paid internships in business and industrial settings (1987). He said that because of their experiences the teachers give their students better information on career opportunities, become more competent and more motivated, improve their instructional methods, increase their earnings and are more likely not to leave teaching, become vehicles through which employers can improve the overall quality of education, and are a source of reliable summer help to corporations.

Gold and his colleagues at the National Institute for Work and Learning, who studied internships in 10 cities, came to conclusions about what made them work. According to Gold (1987), these should be the essential conditions upon which internships in business for teachers are based:

- Business leaders committed to working with schools.
- Employers willing to devote modest staff resources to the organization and ongoing coordination of the internship program.
- Financial backing for high-quality staff members to administer programs and conduct summer seminars in connection with the summer internships so that they are learning experiences and not just summer jobs.
- Universities that cooperate by granting academic credit for the internships and offering ongoing professional development to the internees after they return to their classroom assignments.
- Teachers willing to participate in internships and school systems that encourage them to do so.
- Program administrators sophisticated in education/employer collaboration.

These conditions, however, seem likely to be achieved only under optimal conditions. One obstacle is that unless a business is prospering, its executives may be loath to add to the payroll, especially when the hiring may not lead to greater productivity. Thus, internships for teachers are at the very margin of the outlays that business is likely to make, and internships cannot be expected to be made available in large numbers. In San Francisco, for instance, Ron Eddy, executive vice president of Wells Fargo Bank, said that because some 20 of the city's major corporations have been absorbed, merged, or relocated in the last few years the prospect for internships was dim. Certainly internships are worth pursuing and hold promise for empowering teachers. But it is unlikely that there will ever be enough internships to accommodate more than a tiny portion of the more than two million schoolteachers in the country.

A type of assistance that business can offer teachers at less expense is that provided by playing a role in inservice education. In St. Louis, for instance, where CHART was concerned with international education, the project was able to enlist employees of such multinational corporations as McDonnell Douglas and Monsanto to address the teachers about the issues and cultures of the countries in which they had worked. One program of this sort exposed the teachers to thinking about

Latin American debt, and another focused on transfer of technology. Such information complemented the more theoretical knowledge likely to be imparted by professors.

Perhaps one promising avenue for cooperation might be a coordinated drive by business to encourage employees who are retiring to take part-time and full-time jobs as public school teachers. With the pensions they would get from their companies they might not be concerned about the drop in salary. A survey by the National Executive Service Corps (1987) found that 70 percent of highly skilled professionals in industry would consider teaching after retirement. The survey also circulated among military officers and found that 80 percent of them would be receptive to teaching after retirement. Former military officers and retired business executives are accustomed to bureaucracies, but they also are used to wielding authority within a bureaucracy. They might be good allies in the schools in helping veteran teachers recognize ways of gaining greater power in their jobs.

In any event, businesspeople increasingly are open to contacts with teachers, and access to them certainly raises the possibility of teachers gaining the confidence and encouragement to flex their own muscles. "We all need to know that someone cares, and now we are trying to let teachers know that and to provide an empathetic ear," said Gerald D. Foster, vice president of Pacific Bell and former chairman of the Los Angeles Educational Partnership. "I find teachers to be very social and to have a strong need for recognition from other adults."

Foster would like to see a consensus develop around the goals of education. "If we can get the education community to accept some accountability for defining the product and how students will perform after they complete school, that is a start," he said. "Wouldn't it be nice if the principal let the teachers participate in setting these goals?" Such an outside agency as the Los Angeles Educational Partnership, according to Foster, can be most effective by picking areas for change and hoping that after it begins operating in those areas, the school administration will institutionalize the program and move even deeper into those areas to promote change. "LAEP can't educate the kids," Foster said. "We have to find the niche where the system is ready to change, where it has lost stability and is looking to restore it." In this way business might help open some of the doors to power so that teachers can move in to fill the void.

Despite the flurry of interest in recent years it is still not clear where the collaboration of business and the schools is headed. Business certainly realizes it has a vested interest in improving public education. This responsibility was barely acknowledged at the outset of the 1980s.

But some of the businesspeople most devoted to this agenda worry that in just a few years their companies may be ready to move on to other community priorities, especially if executives do not see marked improvement in the public school systems they have been trying to aid. "Corporations don't like to deal with insoluble problems, and the problems of school systems tend to be insoluble," said Standard Oil's Sondra Hardis. "I'm scared that in a few years the corporations may abandon the public schools."

Teachers were in the schools before business discovered the schools, and they will be there long after business has departed for more verdant pastures, if that is how the scenario plays itself out. The teachers welcome the new interest, but they are largely reserving judgment on its significance. If business decides that it wants to see teachers have a greater say in the operations of schools, then surely the cause of empowerment will gain a powerful ally. That has not yet happened, and it may never occur given the fact that so many corporations do not espouse such a philosophy for their own employees—a fact that has been pointed out more than once in the many books explaining why workers in Japan, whose opinions are solicited by management, are more devoted to quality than those in the United States.

5 ▶

ACCESS TO POWER

THE LEVERS of power, the switches that are turned on and off to make a school system run, are seldom in the hands of teachers. Sometimes it seems that even the building custodian has more authority than the teachers. If teachers are to have greater influence over what occurs in schools, a way must be found to get their hands on the switches that provide access to power. What they need, along with status and knowledge, is access to power.

Schools are riddled with failed attempts at improvement involving teachers who were sent into the fray with lots of empty encouragement and very little backing. In other words, teachers need the support of administrators, as well as the encouragement of movers and shakers outside the schools, to exert influence. In Los Angeles, for instance, this was recognized early in the life of CHART. When high schools were invited to submit proposals for participating, the selection committee tried to eliminate the schools at which the principal did not show clear indication of support for the program. "Some schools were not selected because the committee thought the team did not have the principal's support," said Sheila Smith, a school system administrator in Los Angeles.

The history of the project in Los Angeles is a textbook demonstration of how the step-by-step implementation should be accomplished in a way that gives administrators a stake at each interval — most likely ensuring their support for the ultimate program. Administrators in Los Angeles admit flat out that they fell in line and backed the project because of their perception that their bosses had given support. Word has to come down from each level so that each administrator will know that the one above is committed to the venture. A middle-level administrator in one city said it was when his boss met with a foundation executive that he and other middle-level administrators knew they ought to start backing the foundation's project. "To us," he said, "that was the signal that we should clear our calendars to do everything asked of us to support the program."

In Los Angeles, the commitment to CHART extended to the point that the superintendent offered not to move any more of the principals at the participating schools after having reassigned one of them. The superintendent acknowledged, after the potential problem was brought to his attention, that the project could be jeopardized by the further removal of sympathetic principals early in the life of the project. A new principal, after all, would have less of a stake in a program started by a predecessor.

This concern for showing support for what teachers are trying to do extends far beyond CHART, of course. The superintendent of the Fairfax County public schools in northern Virginia, outside Washington, tried to demonstrate his system-wide backing of teachers by bringing together all 8,300 of them for a pep rally at the opening of the 1986–87 school year, the first time this was ever done. As the tenth largest school district in the country, serving one of the nation's most affluent areas, Fairfax has few of the social problems that confound teachers in urban systems. But even in advantaged districts teachers need overt signs that the administration considers them more than hired hands. "There are three types of people," Superintendent Robert R. Spillane told the assembled teachers. "Those that make it happen, those that watch it happen, and those that wonder what happened" (Karp, 1986).

Officials at the Rockefeller Foundation felt that the backing of a sympathetic superintendent was crucial to the Collaboratives for Humanities and Arts Teaching. It is possible for a program — any program — to go forward, though it probably won't flourish, if the superintendent is ambivalent. But if a superintendent is downright hostile to a program, its chance for survival is nil. Superintendents, on the other hand, are constantly in the difficult position of having to weigh competing priorities in order to select one program over another. And if they opt for a program aimed at empowering teachers, such a decision is fraught with especially heavy implications.

In the case of CHART, some superintendents whose districts participated felt slighted when, upon examining an early draft of this manuscript, they concluded they were not given adequate credit for their contributions. What came across to this author was that superintendents, perhaps no less than teachers, do not feel adequately appreciated. Several superintendents felt they had put themselves on the line in endorsing CHART and that they should be so recognized.

Such sensitivities can, in part, be traced to the precariousness of the

urban superintendency, a job in which the aplomb of a tightrope walker
is as valuable as knowledge of education. The future of the movement
toward teacher empowerment will be immeasurably aided to the extent
that it can show itself not to be inimical to the interests of superintendents. Furthermore, where superintendents do go out of their way to be
helpful, it is clearly important that they get the recognition that they
think they deserve.

Administrations that want to give teachers the freedom to "make it
happen," as Spillane put it, send their message in various ways. In Los
Angeles, for instance, the administration made clear its backing of the
foundation-sponsored Humanitas Academy project by designating
1986–87 as the Year of the Humanities. The principals of the city's 49
high schools could not help but get the message even though the project
was in place at that point in only 8 pilot schools.

"I had always thought that if you want to do something good, you
should close your door and keep quiet about it on the outside," said Neil
Anstead, a Los Angeles teacher, looking at CHART in retrospect and
relating how it had changed his attitude toward administrators. "But
administrators are not so bad and if you take the time to involve them in
what you are doing they can be good." In another city, where the project
did not receive enthusiastic support from the principals, the project
director concluded that one way to stir the zeal of principals was to
change his focus and work through the central administration so that
the principals could see that there was backing for the project by their
superiors.

At some point, whether he or she comes to the decision independently — which is ideal — or as the result of pressure from above, the
principal's backing is vital. A principal who disapproves of a project can
easily sabotage it and combat the teachers' pursuit of power. "The principal of a high school is terribly powerful, and for any project like this to
be successful the principal has to be involved," said Bill Hampton, the
former high school principal. "The principal needs to perceive that
important people outside his school value the project. In the schools
where something is wrong with the project, the odds are that the principal doesn't see the value of the project to the school."

Also, there is another element that is often ignored by those who
would like to change conditions in the schools: the school board. Because they are laypeople whose position is part-time and usually unre-
munerated, there is a tendency to assume that board members do not
matter as much as full-time educators when it comes to winning supporters. More often than not, this is true, but there are enough excep-
tions to the rule to serve as a warning to reformers. In a suburban

district in which the goal of CHART was to boost international education, administrators both in the central office and in the schools seemed
intimidated by the criticism of the project by a school board member.
Though the dissenter was outvoted, his reservations shook the underpin-
nings of the project.

"The word 'international' scares them," a teacher from the suburb
said of the school board. In fact, the board member who was most
opposed to allowing the district to join the project implied that the
venture was subversive because, he said, students who come to think
positively about other countries might end up in certain circumstances
favoring those countries over the United States. Teachers said that to
mollify the school board and reassure administrators who were uneasy
about the idea of such a project, the proposal was rewritten to remove
mention of such words as "black," "global," and "international." "Now,"
said a teacher, "there is no resistance to the project by the building
principal or the department chairman. But they are not asking what
they can do to help either. They simply tolerate it and don't get involved, treating it like nice window dressing."

MISUNDERSTANDINGS BETWEEN ADMINISTRATORS AND TEACHERS

It is remarkable how distrustful administrators and teachers can be of
each other. Perhaps this is a reflection of the limited dialogue that has
occurred in so many schools between the two levels. A teacher who
attended a national meeting that the Rockefeller Foundation sponsored
for teachers and administrators of school systems in CHART said that
the occasion was the first at which he had ever had a chance to speak to
the superintendent in his district, who was also in attendance. And this
was one of the smaller districts in the program.

Administrators generally are not trying to duck teachers. It is just
that the circumstances of their jobs often make it difficult for them to
maintain contact with teachers. Administrators, after all, must spend
time dealing with the community and with the board of education to an
extent unknown to teachers. It is the fact that they are responsible to
several constituencies that sometimes undermines the good relations
that top administrators would like to have with teachers. When administrators are unsure of their support among outside groups, they are less
likely to be firm allies of teachers.

In turn, many teachers are hypersensitive to the opinions of administrators, who may not be aware that they hold as great a sway over the
teachers as they do. Linda Salamon, the Washington University dean

who was a board member of the International Education Consortium that carried out CHART in St. Louis, said that one of her early discoveries in her role was "the teachers' uneasiness about the reaction of their principals. They saw the principals fundamentally as bureaucrats with little interest in anything other than discipline. They worried that the principal would object to their giving up time to learn about ideas instead of marking papers or monitoring the lunchroom."

A veteran teacher in a city where CHART began with little support from the administration offered this observation: "It would be interesting to know the administration's perception of the project. There was no input during the year from the principals. There has been a paternalistic attitude. Teachers are used to being led around by the hand and told what to do. The project could unleash creativity and revolutionize teaching if principals were open and democratic, but, on the other hand, the teachers might find the transition a challenge. After 30 years, I'm skeptical."

In Atlanta, Elease Gates, a social studies teacher, said she saw no increased access to policy making by teachers in her school as a result of their participation in CHART: "They can make suggestions, but those suggestions may or may not be taken seriously," Gates said. "I think principals should have been the ones who attended the institutes before teachers did. Then maybe they would be more receptive to the ideas. I don't think many of the principals really understand what the institute is all about. They just see it as one more thing to come in and disrupt their program."

The depth of the chasm that sometimes separates teachers from administrators was vividly illustrated during one particular interview for this book. The members of the team at a high school participating in CHART unanimously agreed that their efforts to have an impact on their school were being stifled by an unsupportive administration. Yet, when an assistant principal at the school was confronted with this feeling in front of the teachers, he was astounded by the teachers' opinion; he said he thought the school administration was very supportive and that the teachers were satisfied with the backing they were receiving. The separate vantages from which teachers and administrators may view the same situation give them different slants on the role that teachers are playing in a school building or a school system. Administrators who think teachers have been given access to decision making may be truly surprised to learn that the teachers feel as if they are on the outside looking in.

"Teachers don't ordinarily have power because they do not have access to those who wield it." said Arthur Morris, a Seattle teacher. "The way the system is designed, neither the district headquarters nor the principals normally give teachers such opportunities." Teachers are so unaccustomed to gaining power that those in Seattle, for example, could not believe that they really were going to be given authority over curriculum revision through CHART. Jim Grob, the program director in Seattle, said that even after the teachers got involved "they were waiting for the other shoe to drop, waiting for the moment when I would tell them what I wanted rubber-stamped. It took them a couple of weeks to believe they would have power. They have been around long enough to know that that doesn't ordinarily happen."

Similarly, when secondary school mathematics department chairpeople were told by the Pittsburgh Mathematics Collaborative that one of the aims of the program was to allow them to become more involved in decision making in the school system, they were skeptical. They thought, based on experience, that even if they organized around a substantive agenda for action, their involvement would not be welcome. As it turned out, personnel changes in the district's central staff gave promise of a better future for their involvement. Suspicions ran both ways. Some of the projects in Ford's Urban Mathematics Collaborative were viewed with suspicion by administrators who were uneasy about the proposed changes in course structure, textbooks, tests, and teaching methods being considered by the participants, apparently fearing their authority would be undermined (Romberg et al., 1987, pp. 35–36).

Bob Eaglestaff, who participated in CHART in Seattle as a teacher before becoming an assistant principal, thought part of the problem in forging new relationships between administrators and teachers was a perception by administrators that if teachers get more power, it would have to come at someone else's expense. "Where teachers take more control over the curriculum, the general belief is that it means less power for the administration," Eaglestaff said.

Joe Bergin, the English teacher in Philadelphia, had a special vantage from which to view administrative attitudes toward teachers. He was a teacher trainer in a program to help teachers improve their writing instruction. In going into schools across the city to work with teachers, he found that in places where a principal or at least an assistant principal genuinely backed the project and gave leadership to it, the training sessions were successful. By comparison, he recalled one school at which the administration showed no enthusiasm for the program and the principal never made so much as an appearance at the training sessions. Bergin cut the training short at that school, ending it after only five sessions in the belief that without sufficient leadership from the school administration the program was doomed.

Further illustrating the importance of the principal's role in empowering teachers is what occurred in another city, where CHART had difficulty getting schools to participate because principals had received no sign that the central administration desired the cooperation of the schools. "This says to me that their value system downtown is such that they don't value teachers attending conferences," observed a teacher in that city.

The Role of Principal

Examining the possible role that principals can play if they want to be supportive of teachers, Bill Hampton said: "The worst thing a principal can do is be a no-sayer. The principal and the faculty should define goals together and then all the teachers should be encouraged to be initiators. A principal's role is to create a lively environment. Teachers at our school generate their own ideas. They are entrepreneurs. . . . Having the flexibility to leave the building and go to meetings, for instance, is very important for teachers. It gives more dignity to what they are doing. The ability of administrators to control their own time makes teachers jealous. You can't expect teachers to go to meetings only after school."

Teachers readily confirm that the idyllic scenario sketched by Hampton is the sort that would give them greater access to power in their schools and that the principal's attitude is the gauge by which they judge whether they are going to get a piece of the action. "Our principal is supportive of the consortium, and if he weren't we probably could not be as active as we are in the program," said a pair of teachers from a suburban St. Louis school. "He likes innovative teachers and doesn't feel threatened by them. He knows some things work and some don't. When you try to be innovative, he is willing to let you fall on your face. He's a good teacher himself. He not only allows us to leave the building—he even encourages us to." At a school in Los Angeles the teachers said they knew the principal meant business when members of the team designing a new interdisciplinary curriculum were given a joint planning period in addition to their individual planning periods.

Teachers who felt assured of the approval of their principal for a program said they could approach the project in an entirely different manner. Janis Nathan in Los Angeles said that because her principal had been involved in the project "we knew we would not have to go back and sell it to her." This was a reason for the selection committee's policy in Los Angeles of admitting to the project only schools at which officials were persuaded that the proposal had the full-hearted support of the principal.

Support by administrators can be shown in various ways, as was seen in a city where one of the high schools had won a major debate contest. An assistant superintendent and his wife—but not the teachers who had coached the team—were invited to a celebration by business leaders. The assistant superintendent took the two teacher-coaches instead of his wife, and the teachers said it was the first time they ever attended a luncheon at which drinks were served before the meal. For a teacher, access to power means a lot more than getting a cocktail at midday, but that is a symbol of just how far from power teachers have been.

Ideally, collegiality leads to teachers and administrators working together, as partners, sharing power. No longer should teachers have to become principals to have an impact on shaping school policies. The Carnegie Forum Task Force recommended that schools create a professional environment for teaching by giving teachers the discretion and autonomy that professionals enjoy in other fields: "This does not mean no one is in charge, but it does mean that people practicing their profession decide what is to be done and how it is to be done within the constraints imposed by the larger goals of the organization" (1986, p. 39).

A similar philosophy appeared to underlie the deliberations of the National Education Association and the National Association of Secondary School Principals in the preparation of the report, *Ventures in Good Schooling* (1986), which the two groups called "a cooperative model for a successful secondary school." The document contains 84 recommendations on how to encourage cooperation between teachers and principals in such areas as goals, school organization, instruction, supervision and evaluation of teachers, discipline, and the school's relations with families of students. Such a report moves teachers closer to empowerment by acknowledging some of the obstacles in their path and assuaging some of the fears of principals.

On its own, the national secondary school principals' organization launched a program in 1987 to help principals of urban high schools do a better job of drawing their faculty members into instructional decision making. One feature of the program called for veteran principals to serve as mentors to participating principals. Such a program should be complementary to efforts to empower teachers because principals who are more knowledgeable and more confident will feel less threatened in sharing authority with teachers. Yet, there may be just so much that can be done to round off the sharp corners; any instance in which power is exerted is fraught with a basic tension between compliance and resistance (Burbules, 1986).

As it is, many of those who rise to principalships apparently have good reason to be short on confidence since, according to a report by the National Commission on Excellence in Educational Administration (1987), they lack training for the position. The panel, chaired by Daniel E. Griffiths, a former dean at New York University, urged the creation of a national academy to certify principals, somewhat along the lines of the national board that would certify teachers under the Carnegie proposal.

The pursuit of more authority by teachers could easily make it appear that teachers are on a collision course with principals. Indeed early criticisms of the Carnegie Forum's report often centered on the proposal that teachers play a larger role in running schools. The Forum was accused of trying to rob principals of their authority. "That's like running a Cabinet without a President," Samuel Sava (1986), executive director of the National Association of Elementary School Principals, said of the Forum's recommendation that more of a team management approach be used in operating schools. "The report says the principal is a dated concept, but where is the data?" asked Sava. "I thought they were extremely naive when they said the schools of this country can be led by teams. Someone has to be responsible."

In New York City, the principals' union, the Council of Supervisors and Administrators, vigorously objected during the 1986–87 school year to a proposal to let master teachers train new teachers. The union of principals, an affiliate of the AFL–CIO, saw the plan as an intrusion by teachers into supervision and finally voted to file a grievance against the teachers' union, a fellow affiliate of the AFL–CIO. "We already have master teachers working with those entering the system," said Ted Elsberg (1986), president of the principals' union. "They are the principals, assistant principals, and other supervisors who have the preparation, the training, the experience, and the licenses for the job."

In Rochester, the principals' union actually sued in court to block a mentor teacher program that would have given veteran teachers some of the prerogatives traditionally reserved for principals. Some of the same charges were lodged by principals around the country against the recommendation by the Holmes Group that master teachers take on some of the responsibilities usually reserved for supervisors.

Principals have their own agendas and it is perhaps natural that they should protect themselves. Like all middle-level executives, principals tend to be keenly interested in anything that might affect their movement along the executive career path. Principals may not be inclined to support innovations leading to teacher empowerment or other innovations because such changes can increase uncertainty, multiply the complexities of normal school operations, and raise doubts about peer recognition. The bottom line as to whether or not principals or other school officials advocate an innovation "depends on organizational problems and conditions that may make it beneficial, in career terms, for school administrators to innovate" (Pauly, 1978).

It is, of course, foolish to maintain that putting more power in the hands of teachers would in no way diminish the authority of principals. But empowering teachers does not necessarily mean reducing principals to figureheads either. School boards, for instance, clearly continue to regard principals as the ones with the paramount role in running the schools, and that is not likely to change even with greater power in the hands of teachers. An indication of this recognition is the salary of principals, which is higher than that of teachers, although it is worth noting that principals are required to work more days than are teachers. The average principal is paid $47,896 at high school, $44,861 at junior high school, and $41,536 at elementary school, according to the National Association of Secondary School Principals. In other words, principals still are seen as being in charge—if salary has any relationship to the conferring of power. This is not to say that principals are not chafing under limitations on their power. Sarason (1982, pp. 147–49) reminds us that principals feel increasingly restricted by such constraints as court decisions and collective bargaining contracts, not to mention legislative actions and the directives of their own central administrations.

The Role of Teacher

A sign that teachers do not want to strip away all the power of principals is the survey result showing that teachers prefer to work in a school where an able principal is in charge. Schools judged by teachers to be "more satisfying" places of employment were those where the principals were judged to be significantly more in control of their jobs and of their time and where principals felt they had considerable influence. The study, by John Goodlad (1984, pp. 178–79), found that teachers were less satisfied working in schools where principals were less in control and less influential. For their part, many teachers say they are not seeking to enter into a power struggle with principals, but merely want a greater role in decision making. "It's not that we would run over the administration, just that we should have an arrangement that assures us the power to function," Los Angeles's Nathan said.

Pat Cygan, who divided her time in Seattle between teaching and supervising curriculum, observed that not all teachers are particularly eager to be empowered because "they see that administrators are hired to do that, which frees teachers from certain responsibilities." This observation would be in line with the finding in the evaluation of Ford's Urban Math Collaborative Project (Romberg et al., 1987, p. 32) that "the most vexing problem" was that too often teachers expected and received services in a paternalistic manner and were sometimes not all that avid to participate in management and planning. Juanita Morgan, an elementary school teacher in Saint Paul, said that teachers should bear in mind that getting more authority is not without its disadvantages. "With responsibility come burdens," Morgan said. "Until now, teachers could blame administrators for the problems, but that wouldn't be so if teachers had more of the responsibility. It's not that easy, for example, for teachers to take on curriculum development. They may be willing, but they may not have the skills."

So the leadership of principals remains crucial to school success, and if teacher empowerment simply cuts away the autonomy of principals without providing for a new form of healthy shared leadership, the surgery will not cure the patient.

A contribution of CHART toward encouraging cooperation between teachers and principals might be its use as a model of giving some teachers higher salaries for work in which they accept greater responsibility. The arguments about merit pay and career ladders often hinge on semantics. There is no dispute over the practice in higher education of paying professors more than associate professors, and associate professors more than assistant professors. Why could schools not follow a similar pattern and use differentiated responsibilities to justify salary differences? The Carnegie Forum's Task Force has already suggested the idea of having a "lead teacher," so identified by evidence of competence.

Bringing Together Principals and Teachers

Given the new ideas for empowering teachers, where does that leave principals during the empowerment process itself? Should they be part of the program by which teachers are empowered? Should they be participants in these various ventures intended to raise the status of teachers, make teachers more knowledgeable, and build networks by which teachers can exert their influence? It is, after all, in the interest of teachers—not to mention students—to promote the intellectual development of principals. Too often, principals are simply managers, not leaders and perhaps not conversant enough with ideas to make the contribution they might make to the instructional program. Such shortcomings certainly seemed to be on the minds of the members of the National Commission on Excellence in Educational Administration when they recommended that there be new methods for training principals.

Nonetheless, the tendency in most teacher enrichment programs is to limit most aspects to teachers. The reasoning is basically twofold: Not only are the needs of teachers different from those of principals, but the entire tone of the program might change if principals participated alongside teachers. The spark of camaraderie might never be ignited among the teachers. After all, who wants the boss around? The ambiance that characterized the summer seminars of CHART and the sense of community that carried into the school year might have been more difficult to achieve if principals had been part of all the activities. Teachers might have felt they were once again being rated by their supervisors. Candidness might have been restrained and the teachers might not have gained the sense of ownership of the program that it was essential for them to feel. It was this very need for independence that caused the National Education Association in the early 1970s to ask administrators to leave the organization so that it could stand clearly as a group for teachers.

Unfortunately, the history of principal–teacher relationships is so paternal and hierarchical that principals most frequently end up in dominating roles. There has been an unfortunate tendency by some principals to treat teachers as though they occupied a niche only slightly above that of the students they teach. Some principals certainly have the manner and self-assurance to be more equal partners and put teachers at ease, but others might find it difficult to do so. And the spirit that is created among teachers in an empowerment program might be undermined by the participation of principals. It was that spirit that became the core around which the teachers' feelings of empowerment grew, like a snowball rolling downhill, gathering momentum as it descended.

On the other hand, excluding principals closes off the possibility of forging closer ties with them. Bill Hampton, the former principal, said that a solution might be to have a separate, parallel program of seminars for principals so that they could explore the same topics as the teachers and at least build stronger links to other principals. A possible model for this approach could be the one-year training program that the Maryland State Department of Education sponsored. That program was followed by the creation of the state's Institute on School Improvement and Staff Development to enable those who had participated in the training program to continue their learning and possibly become change agents in their own schools. It also helped the principals build the kind of network with each other that would nurture and sustain them.

All of this is not to say that it is impossible for principals and teachers to engage jointly in professional development activities. In Philadelphia, for example, some principals participated in at least a portion of the CHART activities, side-by-side with teachers; this also happened in some other cities. Principals often were required to attend the early sessions in order for their schools to be accepted into the program. Other principals participated even more fully, joining teachers as fellows in the seminars. "For the first time in history," said Judith Hodgson, the program director in Philadelphia, "principals sat down next to teachers so that they could learn together."

BUILDING NETWORKS

But it may be more important, first, to put teachers in touch with each other if they are to be empowered. Contact with the principals can come later. The degree of change in schools is strongly related to the extent to which teachers interact with each other, a factor that has been verified repeatedly (Fullan, 1982, p. 121). As has already been mentioned, part of the powerlessness of teachers is a function of their isolation. Good communication among teachers breeds power. When the monks kept a monopoly on reading during the Dark Ages, it gave them considerable power over the illiterate masses. When teachers always go their separate ways, it adds to their disenfranchisement. The networks that are formed among teachers are a potential avenue of power. Dale Mann of Teachers College, who was an evaluator for Impact II, recalled how it had struck him that the program was something more than it first appeared. "It was clear," he said, "that what I had missed was the difference between a minigrant program and a networking program. It turned out that the minigrant is the bait and the hook is the network — building a whole different set of relationships with other teachers."

Judith Warren Little confirmed the value of networks in the *American Educational Research Journal* (1982) with her finding that successful schools, more than unsuccessful ones, were places where teachers valued and participated in collegial activities. They pursued a greater range of professional interactions with fellow teachers or administrators, including talk about instruction, structured observation, and shared planning or preparation. In the successful schools, they did so with greater frequency and with a greater number and diversity of persons. Also, they did so at locations beyond the school, for example, visiting other schools and attending conferences. Similarly, Fullan found the degree of change strongly related to the degree to which teachers interacted with each other, maintaining that "virtually every research study on the topic has found this to be the case" (1982).

The power that flowed from the network was seen by many as the most vital feature of the Urban Mathematics Collaborative sponsored by the Ford Foundation. Learning to share and discuss mathematical ideas was the most obvious outcome of the project for teachers (Romberg et al., 1987, p. 24). Participants in CHART said the same thing. "The biggest benefit is coming in contact with people from other schools and trading information with them," said Lary Baker, a teacher in the Clayton District, outside St. Louis, who participated in CHART. The power of the group was a main dynamic of these programs. Networking is a word overused in the 1980s, particularly in the business world, but hardly a better word exists to describe this phenomenon.

Thus, teachers have much more chance of gaining access to the mechanisms of power if they can operate as part of a network—a network of like-minded teachers within a school and within a school system and even with colleagues in other districts. It is no revelation that there is strength in numbers, and, clearly, having a team of teachers involved in trying to produce changes at a school is a more powerful prod than using individual teachers. New knowledge and fresh applications have their best chance of taking hold in a climate in which several teachers are similarly enthusiastic and bond together. They can turn to each other for support. So eager are teachers for this kind of experience that when the New Orleans Mathematics Collaborative held an organizing meeting 106 of the district's 150 math teachers showed up.

The power of the group and the esprit de corps it generates are vital. This is why the CHART projects that involved teams of teachers from the same school, rather than individual teachers in each school, seemed to carry more promise of having a deeper impact. Otherwise, proselytes can return from their conversion experience on the road to Damascus only to discover no one is interested in the Good News.

A measure of success of a particular project is the degree to which the network can be extended beyond the original participants. Enthusiasm, unlike the common cold, is not easily spread, and a reinvigorated teacher may find that colleagues, caught up in their day-to-day problems, feel threatened by all that zeal.

Two teachers trained in a program in one city and told to go back and train their fellow teachers recalled that they returned to their school to find that their suggestions were greeted with cynicism and resentment. A team of two was not a large-enough cadre to be a change agent.

A larger wooden horse was needed in this particular Troy. "We would call meetings and no one was interested in attending," recalled one of the teachers. "They would laugh at us."

Roy Lobel of Midwood High School in Brooklyn said that the key is the willingness of the rest of the teachers, who were not involved in the training, to use the returning teacher as a resource. "If you go back and don't have a chance to do anything about what you learned, then teacher empowerment ended on August 5." Marie Collins of Los Angeles said the interdisciplinary project that worked with teams of four or five teachers per school "gave us clout. If there is just one teacher involved, then that teacher can be ignored. Even those of us who individually have been assertive are more empowered by being part of a team. After all, you get tired of fighting the good fight alone." Collins once had the experience of participating in a National Science Foundation institute at Rutgers University in New Jersey and coming back with ideas that no one wanted to hear about. "You come back excited," she said, "but you are still only one person trying to take some of that wonderful stuff back. You left the other 49 people back at Rutgers and they are not there to help you. If we had been a team returning to the school, there would have been a chance of influencing the rest of the school."

Jim Grob, the director of CHART in Seattle, described the potential for networking in his city: "Thirty-five to thirty-eight of the system's eighty world history teachers have now been involved to some extent with the curriculum development. If you add those who took seminars during the year, the number rises to more than half of all the world history teachers in the city. And it has radiated throughout social studies with those outside world history and those down through the middle schools having attended seminars. . . . In another two years, all fifteen units of the new world history curriculum will have been designed, completed, and piloted through two revisions. You will have a teacher-developed world history program, and the next step will be to select the text from the point of view of the program that has been built into the curriculum. . . . I'm not saying that the teachers are the only ones who know anything and that the keys to the school district should be turned over to them. Teachers want support, assistance, and guidelines from the administration. There has to be a balanced marriage."

6 ▶▶

KEEPING IT GOING

SOME TEACHERS in Saint Paul were at only their second conference on the teaching of writing sponsored by Compas with a grant from the Rockefeller Foundation and they were already talking about whether the program could last beyond the funding. Though the discussion was premature since the promise of funding would carry it through another two and a half years, the teachers' concern was nonetheless appropriate. Amid the early euphoria of a successful experience it is easy to forget how quickly the impact of a project can fade if provisions are not made to ensure its continuation. In the case of CHART and its effort to empower teachers, it was not just the funding that was at issue, but whether a whole network of fragile connections could be sustained over the long run.

Such questions are especially relevant in education, a field that has had enough panaceas to produce a new Eden. Innovation after innovation has appeared only to fizzle and expire in a short time. Sometimes the problems of teaching and learning have proved intractable, and yesterday's reform became today's failed pilot project. One difficulty perhaps is that often little attention is given to nurturing a particular reform once it has been set in place. And, like seeds planted in an untended garden, the promising changes are soon overtaken by the weeds of the status quo, and the next time anyone looks nothing seems different. A landmark study of 293 federally sponsored projects in schools in 18 states found that successful implementation did not guarantee long-run continuation and that few districts planned for the long-term stability of the projects (Berman & McLaughlin, 1978).

In any program that lifts the aspirations of teachers there must inevitably be consideration of whether the school system can deliver on its implied promises. Like the person who orders merchandise out of a slick catalogue only to discover that the item that arrives scarcely resembles the description, teachers who do not get the goods they are led to expect may feel demoralized and even betrayed. Dennis Lubeck, who headed CHART in St Louis, observed that such failure by a school system to follow through "could breed dissatisfaction." He went on: "I've become an employment agency for some of these teachers. They go back into their buildings all fired up and find out their principals don't give a damn and their colleagues don't understand what they're talking about. The culture of the school is fundamentally anti-intellectual. You have some teachers who care only about why the last salary increase was not large enough, people who want to teach their five hours and get home as fast as they can."

If there is going to be change that leads to better education, then teachers themselves will have to be agents for that change. Otherwise it is not likely to happen. And it will not occur overnight. Change, in schools at least, is not a one-time event that happens and then leaves everything altered for eternity. Rather, change is a process that takes place gradually over a period of time (Fullan, 1982, p. 115), not like an earthquake that rumbles for a few seconds and then is completed.

Mutual adaptation can be a key in bringing about change (McLaughlin, 1978). What this means is that there has to be a little bit of give all around. Teachers, administrators, school board members— anyone associated with the implementation of the project—has to be flexible and do some compromising. Even the project itself has to be subject to some modifications to make it acceptable to the key players. Adaptive educators are, in effect, "self-renewing," having the ability continually to adapt to the external or internal environment in ways that strengthen the schools and the educators themselves, ultimately helping to improve education (Miles & Lake, 1967). McLaughlin maintained that mutual adaptation, deciding to be a participant rather than a spectator, provides the best chance for success. Otherwise, he wrote (1978, pp. 20–21), there is likely to be co-optation, in which the project appears to be adopted but the appearance is an illusion and nothing actually changes. Or else, there is simply nonimplementation, in which the mechanism breaks down or the project is altogether ignored by those upon whom change is incumbent.

Change can be against the wishes of the administration and even may put one teacher at odds with others. When Neil Anstead helped start the interdisciplinary magnet program at Cleveland High School in Los Angeles, he hoped that the competition from a program that would be rigorous and demanding for the students who spent part of the school day in it would put pressure on the teachers who dealt with the youngsters the remainder of the day. Because the students in Anstead's magnet program were being trained to ask tough questions, he thought this habit they were acquiring would be carried by them into other classes that were not part of the program. While there was some spillover to the whole school, Anstead said he discovered that many teachers outside the magnet program did not welcome the intellectual aggressiveness that the students had learned in the magnet. These teachers, according to Anstead, were past the point where they appreciated being challenged by their students.

The evolving process of change — if it is to last — ought to be accompanied by shifts in attitude so that teachers and supervisors are not only doing something differently, but are coming to believe in it as well. This, too, takes time. If only behavior is altered and attitudinal change does not follow, chances are that teachers will revert to their prior behavior. The process of change could be seen in the experience of Lieselotte Tschesche, a teacher in Saint Paul who was in CHART. "I was drafted into the program by my principal and I was a reluctant participant," she said. "I was skeptical because I couldn't see how I would profit from it. But I have changed my attitude completely. I am a poor writer and I would like to be able to express my thoughts. I got all those activities from the program for getting myself and my students started as writers, and I found myself able to sit and write for 20 minutes at a time. We were enriched with ideas, and I saw how I could apply the ideas to help students write in social studies."

One explanation for the failure of teachers to take more of the initiative for change may have to do with the restraints that teachers impose on themselves. They are so accustomed to doing without power that they may overlook some of the possibilities open to them. The former school superintendent in Los Angeles, Harry Handler, thought there was more latitude for teachers to assert their independence, for instance, than is commonly recognized — even by the teachers. He observed: "There are constraints that are real, ones that are a function of board rules and policies and contractual considerations. Then there are constraints that are truly imaginary, that take on a life of their own. The distance from this office to the classroom is overwhelming. If you're fortunate enough (as a superintendent) to work with a board that supports some of the same things as you and build on that, you can change the reward structure. Once you get teachers to change their perception of what is expected, you start changing behavior."

It is too early to tell whether the changes wrought by some of the recent attempts to empower teachers will last. To be sure, there are likely to be at least temporary benefits for teachers who have enjoyed a boost in status, fortified their knowledge base, and helped shape curriculum, but the very word "empowerment" suggests the expectation of something enduring. The system itself must change in ways that allow these programs to become as much a lasting part of a teacher's way of life as the lesson plan or the chalkboard. This is a large order.

While CHART provided a blueprint for beginning the process of change and represented a knock on the door to empowerment, one cannot easily be sanguine about the long-term impact. "I'm skeptical of us getting into decision making," said Linda Swinko, a science teacher at Lincoln Intermediate School in Cleveland, where Ford's math program and Carnegie's science program were used to upgrade teachers. "There is just too much bureaucracy in the school system, and it takes too long to get through the red tape. The Collaborative is the only place in which teachers are being asked what they want. Unless that kind of approach becomes institutionalized in the school system I can see it just fading away."

Surely some permanent change would be more likely if a foundation or some other outside agency contributed enough money each year to make possible on an ongoing basis the range of activities that occur in ventures such as CHART, or the Urban Math Collaborative, activities that are very much a prod to empowerment. But no foundation is likely to do this because foundations regard their grants as "seed money," funds to get new life sprouting that then must be sustained by others so that the foundation can go on to invest in fresh possibilities. The Yale–New Haven Teachers Institute is one of the few programs that has moved toward keeping itself going after the foundation funding ends, by creating its own endowment. But this would be more difficult for an entity without the advantage of "Yale" in its name.

CHART expended $4,279,000 of Rockefeller Foundation money from 1983 to 1987. Only a small portion of teachers in most participating districts directly benefitted from the funds in terms of stipends and the more alluring features of the program. "It is very expensive per capita," conceded Linda Salamon in St. Louis. This is not to say that Rockefeller was alone in supporting these projects. A goal was to encourage a multiplier effect, and the recipients used the recognition to seek funds from local foundations, corporate donors, and the school districts themselves. In fact, of the $3,609,800 expended by the CHART projects in the 1986–87 school year, only $1,107,800 was from Rockefeller.

In addition, local sources contributed such nonfinancial support as facilities for meetings, consultation, dinners, and materials. Rockefeller had hoped to bring about this sort of fiscal collaboration, and, indeed, it may continue to flow from local sources for quite some time. On the other hand, funders do have a habit of finally ending their involvement in a project and going on to new enterprises. If outside money then is not available for such outlays, how is such a program to survive?

INSTITUTIONALIZING CHANGE

The most obvious solution is for the host school system to "institutionalize" the program, adopting it and funding it out of tax levy funds in the same way that the school system pays salaries and buys books. Given the conflicting priorities in the public schools, this is not a goal easily attained, and even if it were, there is some question of whether institutionalization is in the best interests of a program aimed at empowerment. This is the dilemma. Without institutionalization that incorporates the empowerment principles of the program into the inner workings of the school system and expands on those principles so that the role of teachers is truly changed, it is questionable whether there can ever be full empowerment. But if such institutionalization occurs, there is grave danger of the program being co-opted and absorbed into the school system in a way that so dilutes it that the newly acquired power might be an empty victory.

Could a program empower teachers in the same way if the school system itself were running it? Could the results be the same without the involvement of an outside agency that seems to keep the program "pure" and beyond the "clutches" of the school system? On the other hand, does being effective depend on having the almost pristine quality that comes with outside oversight? And can a program aimed ultimately at empowerment really achieve its objective if it does not become embedded in the heart of the school system's operations?

These are questions that cannot be answered yet, but they do suggest that some very real safeguards must be part of any program to empower teachers that is run by the school system itself. Clarissa Banda, a Los Angeles teacher, worried that "institutionalization under the school system could be the death knell for the program." Short of authentic institutionalized change that results from a full commitment on the part of the school system, there are three possible paths that could be followed if projects are placed under the district's aegis: pro forma continuation that involves going through the actions without real involvement, isolated continuation that limits its survival to pockets here and there, or discontinuation (Berman & McLaughlin, 1978, pp. 19–21).

Even if aspects of programs developed under the aegis of outside agencies are institutionalized into the school systems there will continue to be a function for the outside agencies. Like the think tanks in Washington that act as hothouses for the development of ideas that eventually work their way into the apparatus of the federal government, the outside agencies have demonstrated their permanent value to public education. One way they may begin doing more to help teachers reach further into the recesses of power would be to start giving teachers support to conduct their own independent assessments of their schools and of the school systems. Using established research procedures, teachers and those they hire as their consultants might accumulate information about the working of the schools that would enable the teachers to make their own research-based recommendations for improvement. Congress does something like this through its own investigative arm, the Government Accounting Office, so that it has an independent source of data and is not entirely reliant on information provided by the administration in the White House. Teachers also could gain by this technique. Nothing is a more powerful lever than information.

Having independent information and their own sources of contact can be valuable to teachers (Barnett, 1984). Teachers who have to depend on administrators to keep them informed are at the mercy of the administrators. But if power is seen as "influence potential," it is possible to have power by either being an expert or having access to information perceived as valuable to the group (Hersey et al., 1979). Barnett pointed out that teachers who have power tend to be those in such positions as department chairs because they are more likely to be plugged into the information sources. But teachers in general could change the balance by cultivating their own sources. Then the teachers would be more independent and might even be depended on by administrators for information. This kind of information might be about how to get things accomplished, who to see to solve a particular problem, or what curriculum and classroom materials are available (Barnett, 1984). This notion was embedded in the Rockefeller and Ford programs.

There is also the separate question of how to extend a program beyond the involvement of the core of administrators who originally committed themselves to it and made it prosper. The contacts established at the outset and the support garnered from ranking administrators—the superintendent, middle-level central administrators, and building principals—are crucial to setting up a project that works with teachers. But what happens as the supervisory leadership of a school or a district turns over? How can there be assurance that the new administrators will lend support to a project that is identified with the policies of their predecessors? There is, in fact, a tendency among leaders to want to have programs of their own making, a feeling that the best way to leave one's mark is by a distinctive imprint of one's own, not by keeping the ink wet on something someone else has signed.

If the turnover in staff means that principalships are always in flux, especially in a big city district, there is that much more reason why those who run the projects must continually try to expand the base of support. Otherwise programs intended to alter circumstances for teachers will face the complication of working with principals who do not take the actions they should to abet the process. As it is, half the elementary school principals surveyed by the Association of Supervision and Curriculum Development (1986) said that teachers are never provided with incentives and rewards to change their instruction, even though 92 percent of the principals thought this was important or very important.

GETTING TIME TO BE EMPOWERED

Two of the main issues surrounding teachers and their ability to be change agents have to do with the use of their time and the extent to which teachers shape instructional philosophy and content rather than have it dictated to them. Administrators must be certain that teachers get the space and time to plan and to institutionalize the changes, which, of course, means overcoming their resistance to change (Henson, 1987). The report on the second year of the Urban Mathematics Collaborative (Romberg et al., 1987, p. 30) pointed to the link between time and empowerment with this observation: "If teachers are to become real partners in a reform effort (which would involve developing materials, testing them, and discussing ideas with others), they will need time to plan, to develop, to reflect, and to evaluate."

Empowerment that flows from such changes as being able to leave school for workshops and conferences, working cooperatively with colleagues, and getting involved in planning and decision making cannot realistically rely on hoping that a teacher will make available spare time. If a school system does not deem such activities sufficiently important to set aside part of a teacher's regular school day for them, then that in itself is a statement of how such activities are regarded. "It's unrealistic to think that teachers will have the time to teach and plan unless they are relieved of some of their teaching duties," said Pat Cygan in Seattle. "Curriculum planning can't come on top of a full teaching load." A teacher in Saint Paul who was participating in CHART said that when she asked her principal for time to meet with other teachers in the school during the school day so that they could plan together, she was told there was "no time available for that."

There has to be some reconfiguration of a teacher's time to allow more time out of the classroom. Almost all professionals who work in schools have the same complaint about how little time there is to do anything extra. Two faculty members of the University of Missouri–Kansas City who took leaves to work in public schools discovered that the demands on them ate up the time that they thought they would have available for activities to promote change among faculty members. "No matter how well we organized our public school work, it was largely controlled by the needs of others," they wrote, pointing out that at the university they were used to having considerable control over their time.

One reason CHART had difficulty getting started in Atlanta was because principals were reluctant to give released time to teachers to attend sessions. Paradoxically, releasing them occasionally for professional development is perhaps one of the main ways to keep talented teachers in the classroom. If they are allowed to grow without having to give up teaching altogether, they will remain teachers and not seek the administrative appointments that until now have usually been the only routes to power and higher salaries. Alonzo Crim, the Atlanta superintendent, suggested that perhaps one solution might be eventually to make the teaching schedules of schoolteachers, particularly at the secondary level, more like those of professors. For instance, if a high school English class met three times a week for an hour and a half each session instead of five times a week for forty-five minutes a session, the students would end up with more class time and the teacher would be freed for nonteaching activities for at least an hour and a half twice a week.

But just to show that nothing is easy, teachers who were part of the Pittsburgh Mathematics Collaborative objected to leaving class even when arrangements were offered to make this possible. The teachers said their students needed them, and they turned down the chance to have substitute teachers so that they could have released time during the school day for Collaborative activities. So the program had to be carried out after school, on days off, and on weekends.

An interesting sidelight on the perception of the Pittsburgh teachers comes from the students of the elementary school teachers in the New York area who were released from classes to participate in the Institute for the Advancement of Mathematics and Science Education. The youngsters were asked to write papers about their teachers not being available to them, and their feelings ran the gamut. "I had a weird feeling when she first left because I didn't know who we would have. Now we have a sub that is just as sweet and wonderful as Mrs.

Levow. It's just like having her here," wrote one youngster. Another student wrote: "I feel badly about Mrs. Barry going to school because too much stress is being put on her. She has no time for us because she has too much studying to do." All of which demonstrates just how difficult it is to arrive at the right formula for changing the working conditions of teachers.

Some sort of reconfigured structures are needed in schools for empowerment to have its greatest impact on teaching and learning. New staffing patterns, differentiated salary schedules, new ways of developing and implementing curriculum, reorganized secondary schools that give students the personal attention they need to feel a larger stake in their education—all can be part and parcel of teacher empowerment. Schedules must be rearranged so that some people, while still remaining active teachers, would have assignments leaving time for such duties as teacher training and curriculum writing that are now often handled by nonteachers. Much smaller high schools would be a boon to both teachers and students. Also, career ladders would permit some teachers with differentiated duties to be paid more than other teachers. The existing system not only bodes against empowerment, but also would not allow empowerment to fulfill its potential. New structures would free teachers, letting them make independent decisions about teaching style and giving them the time and freedom to diagnose student needs so that the teachers could then tailor programs for specific students (Fantini, 1986).

In turn, teachers must see themselves as more than mere recipients of services, more than clients upon whom the administration bestows largesse. Teachers cannot be empowered unless they accept responsibility and accountability. Otherwise, teachers are users rather than creators (Common, 1983). "Reformers justify the top-down approach by thinking of teachers as agents and consumers of reform ideas who are powerless, passive, uniform," according to Common. She said that if they are not involved in the creation of the changes so that they have some of the ownership, they will exercise the only power they have: the veto power that is theirs through noncompliance when they shut the classroom door and close out the world.

Examining the effective schools movement, Lawrence Lezotte (1987) concluded that the concept is built on the idea of shared governance and that it assumes that change will come because people inside the schools decide to make the change. If Lezotte's analysis of the concept is correct, then perhaps a reason why the effective schools movement still has not been transformed from an idea on paper to a viable practice is that there is neither shared governance in the schools nor have the people who work in the schools committed themselves to make the changes that are needed.

THE TEACHER'S RESPONSIBILITY

One change in structure that could hasten the advent of more shared governance in schools would be the decentralization of decision making from central headquarters to the school building level. Without safeguards this shift could set up each principal as a little czar, but properly handled it could lead to teachers and principals feeling a bigger stake in their schools and, in turn, committing themselves to make needed changes. Decentralized decision making could be an important step toward greater empowerment of teachers. School-based management is a concept that is mentioned more than it is implemented. It is a bottom-up approach that has the appeal of giving more decision-making power not only to teachers and parents, but to principals as well (Marburger, 1985).

Decentralization of decision making would be of equal value to teachers in elementary schools and secondary schools. While most of the programs described in this book were centered on secondary school teachers, the lessons are generally applicable to elementary school teachers as well. Assuredly there are differences in their circumstances. A teacher at the elementary level is much more wedded to a single class, and the circumstances of that teacher's workday are somewhat different from those of a teacher in a secondary school. The relationship of the teacher and the principal also tends to be different in an elementary school than in a secondary school, where the teachers are not as likely to be infantilized by the principal. But, ultimately, if any move toward empowerment does not reach equally into the ranks of elementary teachers, there could be an unfortunate division between the two sectors, as there was in past generations when high school teachers were routinely paid more than elementary school teachers.

Unions

What role is there in all this for teachers' unions, which have been viewed by such critics as Fantini as obstacles in the path of restructuring — protecting "the ranks of conformity," as he said (1986). One encouraging sign of the role that unions envisage for themselves came when the American Federation of Teachers (AFT) formed a task force in 1987 to examine the extent to which the union's policies and goals were in accord with the school reforms being proposed around the country. There are great consequences in the position that the unions finally take. Such researchers as Susan Moore Johnson and Niall C. W. Nelson (1987) have written that the ultimate success or failure of the reform movement will depend on the reaction of local contract bargaining units. In order to gauge the impact of local bargaining units on reforms, they studied four local districts in which staffing reforms were being addressed. The teachers were not inalterably opposed to changes, but they were much more receptive when they were brought into the discussions at a very early stage and were involved in the continuing talks.

In many ways, collective bargaining and the existence of teachers' unions pose barriers to empowerment in terms of the intransigence that has too often been demonstrated when administrators have sought flexibility in teachers. However, it may be that if there had not been a rise in teacher militancy and if unions had not flexed their collective muscles, the stage would not be set as it is today for new breakthroughs in teacher empowerment (Christie, 1973). Perhaps the old paternalism had to be scrapped and there had to be a more equal relationship between management and employees before management would move on to the next step, empowerment.

Clearly, for needed reforms to occur, teachers' unions must now be flexible in their demands and acknowledge that rigid contractual requirements stifle some possibilities of empowerment, even though the requirements ostensibly protect the interests of teachers. The typical trade union relationship encouraged by the collective bargaining mode that teachers have embraced fosters a worker–management relationship not unlike that in a steel plant or on an automobile assembly line. It was the natural way for the AFT to proceed as a part of the AFL–CIO, and it was the approach that the National Education Association (NEA) tacitly adopted once it dispensed with the niceties of being a "professional organization."

But collective bargaining introduced new elements into the teacher's role and in its early phase clearly earmarked teachers as workers rather than managers. A traditional industrial model of unionism that deals primarily with hours, and salaries may be fine for those employed in factories, but it is inappropriate when the content and composition of the work have so much to do with the outcome, as they do in teaching (Kerchner & Mitchell, 1986). The teacher's own emotional engagement in the job and the teacher's ability to engage the student involve factors that exceed anything likely to be the subject of collective bargaining. Unless unions leave enough room for maneuverability, they will not empower teachers as teachers.

To a great extent, the degree to which teachers gain authority over important decisions in schools will depend on the emergence of a new definition of their role as unionists, as has been conceded in pronouncements by Albert Shanker, president of the AFT. Contracts and interpretations of contracts that tightly constrain the amount of extra effort teachers can put forth may stand in the way of empowerment. While teachers, no more and no less than others, should not be expected to give away their services, their bargaining representatives must be careful about erecting obstacles that, though designed to protect teachers from exploitation, limit the leeway for new patterns of relationships with administrators and restrict the willingness of teachers to redefine their responsibilities.

A model approach is emerging in Pittsburgh, where the Pittsburgh Federation of Teachers, an AFT affiliate, and the city school district have been unusually effective in muting conflict. The two sides struck several agreements that held promise of enhancing the professionalism of teachers. Indicative of the cooperation was a two-year extension in 1985 of a collective bargaining contract that still had a year to run. Included in the settlement was a provision for a Teacher Professionalism Project to deal with a host of issues that went beyond the range of questions covered by the contract. Much of this progress was clearly owed to the ability of Al Fondy, the president of the teachers' union, and Richard Wallace, the superintendent, to view each other as educational partners rather than adversaries. Fondy said: "In our relationships with school districts, while collective bargaining will certainly be maintained and built on, most of the professional and educational progress that we as teachers are going to need to accomplish in the schools will have to be achieved by going beyond collective bargaining in terms of our continuing relationships with school boards and school administrations."

The creation of the Professionalism Project led to the establishment of 11 committees on which teachers and administrators began meeting to consider such issues as the selection of teachers to be instructional leaders in their schools, teacher responsibility for inservice education, and training of newly hired teachers. One of the first agreements reached in committee during the 1985–86 school year provided for a New Teacher Induction Plan to be supervised by panels comprising three teachers and three administrators at each level—elementary, middle school, and high school. The panels were given the authority to monitor new teachers for two years and recommend whether to hire or dismiss candidates.

If the experience with CHART is any guide, there is reason for hope in terms of teachers' unions cooperating with management. In many instances, union leaders were courted as assiduously as were superintendents and principals, and the assent of union leaders was crucial to the operation of the programs. The CHART projects often depended on teachers and administrators being willing to get along.

On the face of it, one might assume that it would be natural for unions to support the empowerment of teachers. But if empowerment is seen by unionists as a ruse for getting teachers to do more work without commensurate pay or if they perceive it as a threat to jobs, they are not likely to be supportive. Where unions have been recalcitrant, critics have sometimes blamed them for the failure of reform proposals. William J. Bennett, the federal education secretary, for instance, charged in 1987 in a speech to the Education Writers Association in San Francisco that teachers were "hijacking education reform and holding it for ransom," demanding raises before they would cooperate with proposals. Whether Bennett was right or wrong, it is clear that union leaders will have to be more conciliatory on certain recommendations.

One of the better examples of the sort of cooperation needed between teachers and administration developed at Staples High School in Westport, Connecticut, an affluent New York City suburb. Acting in response to a state mandate that each local school district create a staff development plan, a committee of two teachers and an administrator at the high school set up staff development grants for small groups of faculty members, who submit competitive proposals for the grants. "We have established a system in which teachers work with other teachers, and it more or less replaces inservice," said Frank Corbo, a mathematics teacher. In many instances the projects involved one teacher taking the lead in aiding in the professional growth of colleagues who agreed to participate in the project. Lis Comm, an English teacher, for example, enlisted eight other English teachers to follow her lead in integrating new works of American literature into their courses, revising course guides, and reexamining teaching methodology used in the courses.

Also more explicitly tied to the teachers' union, the Westport Education Association, an affiliate of the NEA, was another venture, the Teacher Leadership Program, which has been written into the collective bargaining agreement. Teachers submit competitive proposals for one-year grants that augment their pay in an amount equal to as much as five percent of their salary to take on individual projects that involve professional development of themselves and perhaps other teachers as well. Kay Dickstein, for instance, led workshops to teach special education teachers to be better writers so that they, in turn, could improve their teaching of writing. "What this does is empower us to work together in a collegial way," Dickstein said. "It also is empowering to work in a profession you love and to be paid extra to do something so that you don't have to become an administrator to make more money."

The presidents of both the NEA and the AFT seem to share a vision of what is needed for teachers that would go a long way toward empowerment. Speaking of experienced teachers who have given up their careers, Shanker said the real issue was working conditions. "I know that we can't expect the authorities to wave a magic wand and remake our children into highly motivated students," he said. "But they can end adversarial supervision and begin treating our teachers like responsible professionals; they can cut our class sizes to manageable levels; they can clean up our school plants; and they can provide our staffs with adequate material and equipment along with sufficient support personnel to take over nonteaching clerical and custodial chores" (1986).

Mary Futrell, the NEA president, spoke of the growing consensus for putting more decision-making authority in the hands of teachers. "We now have a vast body of research demonstrating that effective schools are schools in which teachers have the latitude and the authority to determine curricular content, craft discipline codes, define schoolwide objectives and goals, and help design standards of teacher certification that ensure the integrity of our profession" (1987).

Yet, if unions want to see individual teachers given greater power so that they may be true professionals, then the unions will also have to be more cooperative in helping school systems deal with teachers who are burned-out or just plain incompetent. It is only fair, as the unions argue, that such teachers initially be given help to improve themselves. But the unions then will have to face up to the fact that some teachers do not belong in their jobs and that they should be dismissed. Giving more power to teachers who perform poorly is not wise and can just make it worse for the students who sit in their classes, as well as for the other teachers whose reputations are lowered. Teachers, like physicians, are terribly protective of incompetence in their ranks. The labyrinth of legal procedures that must be navigated to rid a system of an incompetent teacher is a mockery. There should be a quid pro quo in empowerment, with the teacher organizations finally getting serious about helping school administrators combat incompetence.

Taking Away Power

On the other hand, just because some deficient teachers persist in their positions, all teachers cannot be treated as though they do not know how to do their job. There is an unfortunate tendency emerging to give power with one hand and take it away with the other. This is what some teachers see happening in the trend toward making the curriculum "teacher-proof." A host of new regulations by states and school districts prescribe narrow objectives for students and, in effect, proscribe flexible approaches by teachers who want to respond to conditions as they see them. The students are to be tested each step of the way, and this may leave teachers less latitude in running their classrooms.

As the school reform movement has rolled merrily along, the political atmosphere that helped foster it has led to increased demands for evidence that improvements are indeed occurring. While the goal seems worthy, it too easily lends itself to the kind of simplification that can curtail ingenuity by teachers and force the juices out of teaching. This is anything but empowerment. Frank Smith (1986), in his book *Insult to Intelligence*, complained of programmed instruction that trivializes the curriculum and coerces teachers to take a prescribed approach. He said that where such practices existed, there was what amounted to lack of trust of teachers.

Bernard McCann, a teacher at Ritenour High School, outside St. Louis, said that teachers were "being put in a straightjacket by new state requirements." Another teacher in a neighboring district, Clint Blandford, said: "I'd get out of teaching when the time comes that someone comes into my classroom and tells me how to teach. The more restrictions that are put on the way people teach, the more it will drive people out. It's true that we brought it on ourselves, but the solution is not in prescribing."

Ironically, this move to restrict the professional latitude of teachers comes at a time of mounting interest in upgrading the educational and certification requirements of teachers. It is questionable whether the new breed of teachers being sought would be willing to have their actions subject to such limitations. People who can measure up to higher standards are unlikely to tolerate rigid constraints on the way they are permitted to do their jobs.

What then should happen if empowerment is to have a deep and lasting effect? It is certain that administrators, school board members, and parents must trust teachers to do their job competently if the reins are to be loosened enough for teachers to have the flexibility that will make them more powerful. Trust of teachers is undoubtedly an underlying issue that is not addressed openly. People do not willingly bestow power upon those in whom they do not have confidence. But certainly if society's most precious possession — its children — are entrusted to teachers, there are grounds for trusting those teachers to have more to say about how schools are run.

Empowerment, of course, is not an end in itself. If teachers who gain more power over their work situation do not end up doing their jobs better, then empowerment will mean little or nothing so far as the education of children is concerned. Of what value is greater power in the hands of teachers if it is not used in behalf of the learning of their students? The improvement of learning should be the goal of empowerment.

7 ▶▶

THE PROJECTS

THE VEHICLE that the Rockefeller Foundation used to reach teachers was arts and humanities education. Teacher empowerment could have been sought through mathematics, science, the social sciences, or some other subject area. But the Foundation chose the route it did for very specific reasons. One explanation was the fact that the project was carried out through the Foundation's Arts and Humanities Division. As mentioned at the outset of this book, the inspiration for the program came from the findings of the Rockefeller Commission's 1980 report, "The Humanities in American Life." If the arts and humanities were to flourish in this country, according to the reasoning, more would have to be done to reach Americans while they were still in elementary and secondary schools so that they could be inculcated with experiences and values that would help them enjoy and support the arts and humanities.

Thus was born a program with the unwieldy title of "Strengthening Secondary School Education Through the Arts and Humanities," eventually to become CHART. The hope was that the programs in the various cities would be sufficiently impressive to influence those cities — through a collaboration of the public schools, higher education, cultural institutions, and business — to sustain such activities in the schools without the involvement of the Rockefeller Foundation. The projects started up over a span of several years from 1983 to 1986; Rockefeller's funding cycle was to be completed by 1990, leaving the continuation of the Collaboratives for Humanities and Arts Teaching to local sources.

Rockefeller wanted to ensure that English, history, foreign languages, and the arts were recognized as essential priorities in the schools along with science, mathematics, and technology, which were being swept to ascendancy by the reform movement. As the project has evolved, regardless of its effect on the empowerment of teachers — which, of course, is the major focus of this book — it is clear that it has also had an important impact on education in the arts and humanities. Each participating school system took a different approach, but, collectively, the result is that these are now places in which students are writing more; being exposed to more visual and performing arts; getting a deeper sense of history; seeing connections between history, literature, and the arts that were not previously demonstrated; and being introduced to non-Western cultures that have been alien to them.

In size, Rockefeller's program was but a footnote to the enormous undertaking of the National Endowment for the Humanities (NEH), surely the most important vehicle for promoting such education. This book, in focusing on the Rockefeller program, in no way is intended to diminish the contribution of the Endowment so far as arts and humanities education is concerned. Through its Division of Education Programs, NEH runs its vast project of Humanities Instruction in Elementary and Secondary Schools. For both teachers and administrators there are NEH institutes, usually conducted by colleges and universities, that focus on major topics and texts and the most effective ways of teaching them. There are also collaborative NEH projects to help groups of elementary or secondary teachers who, as representatives of their schools, want to establish a systematic and sustained relationship with a neighboring institution of higher education to improve the teaching of the humanities in the schools.

That CHART was carried out primarily in large urban school districts and with an eye toward empowerment is not without significance. This nation faces a crisis in terms of the education being provided in big city school systems — the largest three dozen of which now enroll one-third of all the black and Hispanic students in the United States. Twenty-three of the twenty-five biggest urban school districts now have a majority of minority students. If a proper grounding in the arts and humanities is denied such students, then it will make it that much more difficult for the arts and humanities to survive and for those students to survive so far as the quality of their lives is concerned. Language, values, and civility, the substance of humane existence, must be transmitted, and young people must embrace and absorb such experiences. The imperative for teaching the arts and humanities is no less urgent in other school districts attended primarily by affluent students. But though the arts and humanities are not faring so well even in some suburban school districts, the situation is not so critical as it is in the urban systems.

All of this is not to say that the ventures under Rockefeller auspices worked to perfection. They did not; there were some fitful starts and failures. But much that was worthwhile was accomplished so far as content in the arts and humanities was concerned, and it is worth looking a bit closer at the individual CHART projects to learn more about how they pursued their goals.

ATLANTA HUMANITIES PROGRAM

The National Faculty is an organization that has spent its life as a matchmaker, putting schools in touch with college professors who are then paid by the National Faculty to advise the schoolteachers and instruct them in studies in the humanities. Several hundred professors around the country are members of the National Faculty, taking on these consultancy assignments in elementary and secondary schools on top of their regular, on-campus work. The organization was a key partner in the Atlanta Humanities Program, marking the first time that the National Faculty took on an entire school system as a client. The agency that had oversight over the program and worked with both the National Faculty and the Atlanta public schools was the Atlanta Partnership of Business and Education. When Ben Ladner, president of the National Faculty, began meeting with Alonzo Crim, the Atlanta superintendent, the timing was right because Crim was in the process of trying to get more humanities into the schools and upgrade literacy skills.

It was decided that CHART would reach into every public high school in the city, working with teachers of the language arts, the social sciences, Spanish, and French. The school district was divided by the project for administrative purposes into three geographic areas with about seven high schools in each. Two project teams were established in each of the three areas, one for language arts and the other for social sciences, with two teacher-members on each team from each of the seven schools. The teams for foreign languages were system-wide, with eight teachers on the French team and eight on the Spanish team because the foreign language departments at the secondary schools were small. In the second year of the program, the 1985–86 school year, a new system-wide team was started in the fine arts, made up of teachers of music, visual arts, and creative arts. The list of participating teachers in the Humanities Program grew to about 130, and almost another 100 Atlanta teachers participated in one aspect or another of the program.

Each project team received four two-day visits from members of the National Faculty. At a two-day workshop, a professor typically spent the first day with the teachers examining subject content. Then, on the second day, there would be an exploration of teaching strategies for conveying the material they delved into the first day. One such workshop, for instance, involved an examination of Mark Twain's *Huckleber-*

ry Finn. The second day, when the teaching strategies were discussed, the professor taught a lesson with a model class. Some of the topics readily lent themselves to an interdisciplinary approach, and multidisciplinary teams of teachers were invited to participate. Other times the topics revolved more precisely around a single discipline.

Contact between the program headquarters and the teachers in the program was handled by a faculty liaison, a college professor assigned by the National Faculty to work with each of the teams. Each faculty liaison was paid to give the team seven days a year of time and, in addition, arranged for other professors to meet with the team as paid consultants on an as-needed basis. The faculty liaisons were professors at colleges and universities in the Atlanta area, laying the groundwork for what was hoped would become ongoing collaboration between the schoolteachers and the professors' institutions. The emphasis was on showing ways in which art, music, and writing could be used in the teaching of English, social sciences, foreign languages, and fine arts. The professors helped teachers understand their disciplines better and assisted them in developing collegial resources using new texts and fresh ideas.

A major component of the program was an institute each summer at the University of the South in Sewanee, Tennessee, which both pulled together the work done in the schools during the previous year and provided a vision of what the teachers could expect from the program in the coming year. The third summer institute in 1987 brought together 125 teachers from Atlanta's public high schools for two weeks of intensive study. Also, for the first time a group of 25 high school students participated in the institute with their own sessions.

For further information about the program, readers may contact: The National Faculty, 1676 Clifton Road, Atlanta, GA 30322 (404-727-5788).

PROJECT FOR INTERDISCIPLINARY HUMANITIES TEACHING IN
SECONDARY SCHOOLS (LOS ANGELES)

The goal of the program, operated by the Los Angeles Educational Partnership in conjunction with the Los Angeles public schools, was to find ways to engage a growing multi-ethnic, multi-cultural student population in meaningful humanities education. This was to be done in a way that brought students to recognize the value of their differences and of the commonalities that link them. Called simply "Humanitas," the project was modeled on an interdisciplinary program at one of the district's high schools.

It began with four-member teams at eight participating high schools and in its second year was expanded both by adding two to four additional teachers to the teams at the original high schools and starting four-member teams at five other high schools. Teachers continuing in the program were paid $500 each, and teachers new to the program were paid $1,000 each. Every participant, old and new, got a $200 minigrant. Additional stipends were available for experienced team members to consult as experts with new teams and for grade-level coordinators in schools. Schools got grants to buy library books for the program and to contact parents in an attempt to recruit new students into the program. The school system agreed to hire substitutes to replace Humanitas teachers during some of the activities in which they were participating.

Teams of teachers were chosen to participate in Humanitas based on the following criteria: enthusiasm at the prospect of interdisciplinary instruction; strong administrative support; expertise in the subject areas of English, history, and art; willingness to do extra work; and a desire to include in the program students from all achievement levels, not just the high performing.

An important feature of Humanitas was the annual summer academy, which in 1987, for example, brought together participating teachers for two weeks at UCLA and then for a half-week at a retreat location. The goal of the summer academy was to provide each team with the time to work together to develop both the overall structure of a year-long interdisciplinary curriculum and the specifics of the units that would be used at the outset of the school year. The rest would have to be done during the year, staying a few steps ahead of the students. The teachers were taught how to coordinate curriculum among disciplines and were introduced to new curricular possibilities, including greater familiarity with the resources of cultural institutes, museums, and colleges in the Los Angeles area.

Formal arrangements were made to enable teachers experienced in the program and those new to the program to meet during the school year and visit each other's projects. There were also two day-long conferences at a college campus for teachers and their students in each of the school system's regions. Other activities during the school year included informal dinners and invitations to cultural events. In addition, every month or so there was a forum at which the team coordinators could share ideas. Two teachers who had gone through the summer program were paid retainers by Humanitas during the 1987–88 school year, one to work in program evaluation and the other to develop cooperative programs that teachers could pursue with museums.

An attempt was made to build collegial links between teachers and college professors with a series of eight three-hour seminars at which those from both levels could gather to discuss topics in the humanities. During the first hour of each seminar, teachers engaged in team planning for the interdisciplinary programs; during the next two hours, there were lectures and discussions with UCLA faculty members. Collaboration grants of $1,000 were available to encourage a teacher and a professor to work together to design and implement a project, a course, or an event to improve humanities education in secondary schools.

For further information about the program, readers may contact: Los Angeles Educational Partnership, 1052 West Sixth Street, Suite 716, Los Angeles, CA 90017 (213-975-1246).

NEW YORK AND THE WORLD

A newly mandated global studies curriculum for the state's ninth graders provided the raison d'être for New York and the World, a training program to help social studies teachers and department chairpeople prepare to implement the requirement for the system's 91,000 ninth graders. The project was a collaboration of Global Perspectives in Education, which is an ongoing organization, the New York City public schools, and various cultural institutions in the city.

The central feature of the program was the summer institute that explored, for one week each, Africa, the Middle East, Latin America, and Asia. Scholars from universities and cultural institutions led the sessions, at which teachers could become more familiar with the regions that now have to be included in their courses. As the regional focus of the summer institute shifted, the site was moved to an appropriate locale, going, for instance, from the Asia Society to the Center for African Art to the China Institute. Lectures were given in the mornings, and afternoons were devoted to curriculum writing and cultural activities.

While the immediate goal of the program was to prepare teachers to conform with the ninth-grade mandate, the larger mission was to expose them to the city's wealth of cultural resources that could enrich their teaching generally. Thus, during the week that each cultural institution was host to the summer institute, there might be dance shows or exhibits of appropriate artifacts.

Material presented to the teachers at the institute was to reflect the core values and unique style of each region as realistically and sympathetically as possible. The idea was to challenge any ethnocentric interpretation of history and cultural studies that might be reflected in school textbooks. The program began its first year by selecting 36 teachers and department chairpeople from 11 high schools and 1 junior high school. The work the teachers did in revising the ninth-grade curriculum became the blueprint for the calendar of lessons produced for the entire school system.

The school system pledged that it would provide paid released time and per session payments for the participants in the follow-up activities during the regular school year. The continuing involvement in the program throughout the year was considered a key element, making it markedly different from the experiences that the teachers had had with previous summer offerings that had no follow-up once school began. It was intended that teachers would remain part of the program year after year, participating in activities long after their involvement in the summer institute.

For the second summer institute, in 1987, 60 teachers from 20 additional schools were added to the program. Afternoon sessions dealing with teaching methodology were led by teachers from the 12 schools in the program the previous summer. Also, plans were made to bring in teachers of English and foreign languages as participants along with the social studies teachers and to enlarge the network of assisting universities and cultural institutions.

For further information about the program, readers may contact: New York and the World, c/o Global Perspectives in Education, 45 John Street, Suite 1200, New York, NY 10038 (212-732-8606).

PHILADELPHIA ALLIANCE FOR TEACHING HUMANITIES IN THE SCHOOLS

Funds allocated through CHART were spent for a wider range of activities in Philadelphia than in any other city, the grants being meant to aid PATHS generally rather than just one or two of its programs. This assistance stimulated major funding from local sources, including Pew Memorial Trust and corporate donors. Through these expenditures it is possible to see the wide array of activities in which an outside agency devoted to promoting humanities in the schools can involve itself.

A key component of the effort was the Writing Across the Curricu-

114 THE EMPOWERMENT OF TEACHERS

lum Program described more than once in the pages of this book. The seed planted by PATHS bore fruit, and by the end of 1986 the school system had absorbed 90 percent of the cost of the writing program and full institutionalization into the school system was expected. The program led to the training of 1,500 teachers a year in 150 schools, with a summer institute for teacher-consultants as a key ingredient. The teacher-consultants were able to go into schools throughout the district during the regular school year to train other teachers because substitutes were provided for them while they were absent from their home schools.

Ten summer institutes were mounted by PATHS during 1985 and 1986 to train almost 200 teachers in literature, languages, and history. Among the institutes were those on contemporary France, decisive periods in Spanish history, the languages and culture of Puerto Rico, Shakespeare, the drafting of the U.S. Constitution, and industrial society in Philadelphia.

Colloquia during the school year offered teachers the chance voluntarily to continue their learning and their networking with colleagues. About 1,000 teachers accepted the invitation and attended sessions on "Treasures of the Rosenbach" at the Rosenbach Museum and Library, "American Social and Cultural History" at several of Philadelphia's museums, "The Golden Age of Islam" at the University Museum of the University of Pennsylvania, and "Who's Afraid of the Avant-Garde?" at Temple University.

Some of the CHART funds, along with money from other sources, wound up in minigrants awarded in 92 schools in response to competitive applications submitted by teachers. Altogether the grants went to 347 teachers whose classes enrolled 11,000 students. Minigrant projects ranged from introductions to literature for elementary school pupils to contemporary poetry in high schools to explorations of local history. Cultural history programs developed through minigrants by teachers at two high schools formed the basis for a system-wide revision of the world history curriculum.

PATHS sponsored a series of one-day meetings on issues related to teaching the humanities in urban schools. A symposium on "Magna Carta" launched a full year of programs on the bicentennial of the U.S. Constitution, with jurists, legal historians, and constitutional historians assisting social studies teachers with curriculum development. Another symposium on "Literature and Literacy" produced printed materials for the district's literature and reading teachers.

Looking ahead, by 1987 PATHS had plans—with aid from the National Endowment for the Humanities—for a program called "Exploring the City, Understanding the Nation: American History Through the Philadelphia Experience." It would reach 180 teachers in 90 schools. Also, PATHS was preparing to develop a program to integrate art history, aesthetics, and practice into major academic disciplines.

For further information about the program, readers may contact: Philadelphia Alliance for Teaching Humanities in the Schools, 400 Suburban Station Building, 1617 John F. Kennedy Boulevard, Philadelphia, PA 19103 (215-665-1400).

CRITICAL THINKING PROGRAM (PITTSBURGH)

The aim of the Pittsburgh public schools, which administered the grant, was to increase the level of discourse and critical thinking in arts and humanities in the secondary schools. Consultants from Carnegie-Mellon University, the University of Pittsburgh, and St. John's College at Annapolis, Maryland, met with the school district staff to plan the program. Discussion was seen as the vehicle to prod students to do more thinking; it was recognized that teachers would have to learn to be adept as discussants if they were to lead such discussions and not merely lecture at students. Furthermore, teachers would need help to show students that writing and discussion were ways of acquiring knowledge rather than just ways of evaluating how much students had learned.

Integration of arts and aesthetic experiences into all subjects was seen as important to the development of critical thinking so as to increase the incidence of higher order thinking in the arts generally and to promote the application of aesthetic interpretation throughout the curriculum. Also, it was seen that "covering" the curriculum was not as vital as identifying key concepts that students should understand and be able to apply. In a Russian history course, for instance, it was preferred that students comprehend the implications of czarist rule on Russia instead of memorizing the names and dates of the reigns of 20 czars.

As the program progressed, students were asked not only to use writing as a way to pursue critical thinking, but also as a way of looking and listening. Visual arts and music were added, sometimes in lieu of philosophical writings, so that students could get a better grasp of how "nonverbal text" can stimulate thought and discussion. In the unit on Russia, for instance, this might mean viewing religious icons or listening to Mussorgsky's *Pictures at an Exhibition*.

A final part of the Critical Thinking Program was to reconsider the assessment procedures so that the ability to evaluate and synthesize would be tested along with the ability to retain information. Thus, the program sought to encourage a synergy among teacher inservice, curriculum, and testing to achieve the various goals.

Teacher training consisted of workshops centered on the use of discussion in the classroom. The program was piloted at Schenley High School, where 65 of the 87 faculty members participated. In turn, the teachers went back into their classrooms and led their students through at least four discussions during a single semester based on brief selections from insightful writings in literature, philosophy, mathematics, and physics. Writings on music and the visual arts are being added. Project staff members observed, assisted, and provided feedback to the teachers. The program was expanded to five more Pittsburgh schools in 1986–87, and teachers from Schenley, who had been trained the previous year, coached their colleagues in the additional schools.

The program initially focused on defining a model of discussion that could be widely disseminated. The teacher's role as discussion leader was different from the typical role in that the teacher had to relinquish some of the control and actually become a "learner" in the group discussion, asking questions only to encourage clarification, elaboration, and support of ideas, not to assess students.

A component of the Critical Thinking Program was the Pittsburgh Symposium: Arts Education as Critical Thinking, intended to expose teachers and supervisors to higher level cognition in various arts areas. The school system's division of arts education went on to seek ways of using art to promote learning in various academic subject areas.

Another component of the program was the Syllabus Examination Project, which was designed to revise the curriculum and devise assessment procedures that would develop students' skills in analyzing major themes and relationships as opposed to dwelling on recall of facts. Attention first was given to the World Cultures curriculum. Some of the facts that had to be taught were eliminated to provide more time in the curriculum to look at larger themes. Tests had to be changed to reflect the altered expectations in the course. New questions framed for students ranged from single-sentence summaries to longer exercises to test both knowledge of facts as well as mastery of concepts and their application. Based on an evaluation of the revision of the World Cultures curriculum, a similar effort was launched in American history and tenth-grade English.

For further information about the program, readers may contact: Division of Research, Testing and Evaluation, Pittsburgh Public Schools, 341 South Bellefield Avenue, Pittsburgh, PA 15213 (412-622-3942).

COMPAS DIALOGUE (SAINT PAUL, MINNESOTA)

Compas, the largest community arts agency in Minnesota, developed Dialogue to supplement a more modest writers-in-residence program that was already in place under its aegis. The principle on which Dialogue's participation in CHART was based was that of long-term association between teachers and writers. The three phases of activity were an institute during which teachers were given an overview of program concepts and approaches to the writing process, an extended residency in the school by a professional writer of usually six to eight weeks spread out over the entire school year, and writing and teaching seminars that met weekly during the residencies, allowing teachers to work on personal writing skills and to develop lesson plans and activities for their students.

Unlike the earlier program, Dialogue set out to put more emphasis on making writers of the teachers themselves, giving teachers the chance to experience what their students would experience as they tried to improve their writing. To this extent, the endeavor resembled the National Writing Project. Many of the teachers found it was the first time they had someplace to turn for this kind of self-improvement. The goals of Dialogue were to aid teachers in learning new teaching skills, to encourage teachers to write themselves, to provide year-long support for teachers, to effect change throughout the school system, and to explore ways to utilize successful components of this model and adapt them to other subject areas. The emphasis was on originality of thought and image, encouraging students — and teachers who wrote — to discover a sense of authorship.

To test this new focus on long-term associations with writers and the idea of making writers out of teachers, a pilot program was conducted by Compas in 1984–85 in the Anoka-Hennepin and North Saint Paul school districts. The Saint Paul district was chosen as the site for the full-blown program the next year. Unlike the Rockefeller programs in most other districts, Dialogue held its institutes on two weekends just after the onset of the school year instead of during the summer. Then there were ongoing activities during the year to reinforce the teachers in their attempts to become better writers. More than 100 teachers took part in the first institute, which was held at Hamline University with sessions taught by poets, novelists, journalists from two local newspapers, and members of the Hamline faculty. Teachers willing to undertake additional writing assignments beyond those required during the institute were eligible for three graduate-level credits in a course at Hamline.

And, of course, the professional writers were in residence at the schools during the year. Writers and teachers worked together in teams and in groups devising new ways to teach writing. There was contact between writer and teacher before each classroom session, though the amount and effectiveness of the planning and debriefing varied according to teachers' interests in writing and other demands on their time and attention. The writers worked directly with students, both independently of the teachers and in collaboration with the teachers. These activities varied from a ninth-grade civics class writing poetry about prejudice to second-grade students moving from group-writing with the classroom teacher to individual poems produced through directed exercises led by the professional writer. Other typical activities were an extensive oral history project in a sixth-grade class that required interviewing, note-taking, drafting, and writing a news article; peer conferencing; and projects integrating the arts and writing.

With the professional writers available in the classroom and the teachers knowing more about how to write, the hope was that ultimately this would translate into stronger writing instruction for the students. As part of the residency, the professional writers would even develop writing groups of teachers, giving them encouragement to look to one another for support in understanding and teaching writing. About half of the teachers in the program agreed to participate in these groups. The three-year program, which included both elementary and secondary schools, began with ten schools, and ten more schools were to be added in each of the next two years. Eight to ten teachers from each school participated.

For further information about the program, readers may contact: Compas, 308 Landmark Center, 75 West Fifth Street, St. Paul, MN 55102 (612-292-3249).

INTERNATIONAL EDUCATION CONSORTIUM
(ST. LOUIS)

The consortium was dedicated to assisting high school teachers of the humanities, the social sciences, the arts, and science to integrate a study of international issues and other cultures into their courses. It did this by identifying interdisciplinary teams of lead teachers from participating schools. They attended programs and had the benefit of consultants who offered workshops and organized seminars and evening programs for teachers with representatives of multinational corporations and college faculty members. The teachers had the benefit of a resource center that published a newsletter, and there was a program to educate administrators about the importance of the humanities and international education.

Teachers from a participating school in St. Louis or one of the surrounding suburban systems attended an annual week-long summer institute on a single international topic and at least two one-day workshops during the school year with multidisciplinary formats and content. The multidisciplinary nature of the endeavor could be seen in 1985 with the first summer topic—Latin America. Teachers of literature, history, science, and foreign languages attended presentations on Latin American history, current politics, contemporary writers, and the impact of deforestation on economic development. The summer topics in 1986 were India and technology; the 1987 topic was Japan.

Teachers were given support throughout the school year in integrating content and methods from the workshops into the curriculum. Consultants from colleges were made available to help teachers create multidisciplinary courses in their high schools, giving advice on both content and teaching strategies. The teachers were also aided in efforts to reach out to other teachers in their schools.

The consortium ran collaborative programs with companies and institutions represented on its board and its advisory panel. For instance, there was a dinner program on doing business in Asia at which the host was Ralston Purina International, a seminar on Latin American literature sponsored in conjunction with Washington University, and a three-day conference on the importance of cultural and linguistic understanding in business held jointly with the School of International Business at St. Louis University.

Shoring up support for the program from school administrators was viewed as a major responsibility by the consortium. Toward this end, it developed a strategy that called for appointing school superintendents to the consortium board, cultivating relationships with administrators in charge of curriculum and staff development, holding luncheons for the principals of participating schools, having an annual lunch for school board presidents and superintendents, and inviting administrators to meetings sponsored by foundations that supported the consortium.

For further information about the program, readers may contact: International Education Consortium, 470 East Lockwood, St. Louis, MO 63119 (314-721-3255).

CROSSROADS SEATTLE

Social studies students in Seattle were to be exposed to more than the Western European cultures that traditionally formed the backbone of their courses. But the aim was to figure out a way of doing this without simply creating the "add-on" units that often were used to introduce new content. Instead, the curriculum was to be rewritten to incorporate this multi-cultural approach. It was decided that the way to do this was through broad ideas or concepts that could be examined, in turn, from different cultural perspectives. Crossroads Seattle sought both to revise the world history curriculum of the school system and to give teachers the knowledge and preparation they would need to teach the new curriculum.

Teachers were joined in summer workshops by university professors who both taught them about some of the cultures less familiar to them and advised them about how a new curriculum could be built around what was being taught. In a sense, the teachers immediately applied what they learned, sitting through classes as learners part of the day and collaborating on the specifics of the curriculum the rest of the day by applying what they had learned. The professor-consultant continued to confer with the teachers about curriculum development during the school year, meeting with them after school and on weekends.

Teams of five to eight teachers divided up the world, each team taking a region and applying the same conceptual questions, using a sort of matrix approach so that similar features could be compared around the globe. In each part of the world, this meant looking at such aspects of the indigenous cultures as their institutions, production and distribution, governance, language, art, world view, and acculturation. Each of these concepts — in each part of the world — was to be studied in terms of facts and statistics, similarities with and differences from other regions, patterns, adaptation to change, justice and equity, and prejudices.

It was expected that in most cases this would lead to study of family, community, nationhood, education, government, legal system, national defense, and agriculture in the particular culture. It could also lead to study of work and labor, trade and transport, income distribution, scarcity, capital, technology, and resource management.

By the second year of its operation, Crossroads Seattle was exploring what it could do to help revise the school system's entire curriculum, from kindergarten through twelfth grade in every subject, to reflect cultural influences other than those of the West. During the summer of 1987 prototypes were developed to infuse such concepts into portions of the existing curriculum in mathematics, reading, health, social studies, and science.

For further information about the program, readers may contact: Crossroads Seattle, Seattle Public Schools, 815 Fourth Avenue North, Seattle, WA 98109 (206-281-6000).

SOUTH CAROLINA HUMANITIES INITIATIVE

The youngest and most unusual of the programs launched under CHART sponsorship was the South Carolina Humanities Initiative, which started in 1987. Its goal was to bring together private and public sector resources and organizations to improve the quality of humanities education in rural public schools. Much of the work of the program was based on overcoming the special problems facing teachers of the humanities in locales where they are isolated from professional colleagues and severely limited by resources and lack of access to up-to-date materials.

Exacerbating the problem in rural schools is the small enrollment that means an equally small faculty with no more than one or two teachers for each subject in the humanities. With few staff members available to develop locally appropriate material and little extra money to buy such materials, rural schools frequently are restricted to using little more than textbooks and do not draw as they might on community experiences that might be the basis for lessons in the humanities. Also, the smallness of the schools and the staff mean that the breadth of offerings in the humanities is necessarily restricted.

Five main objects were set for the program: to develop over a three-year period a group of teachers in rural school districts trained to improve students' reading and writing skills through humanities instruction; to solidify partnerships among rural public schools, colleges and universities, and state agencies to improve humanities education; to create a computer network for humanities instruction and curriculum management; to expose teacher education students to instructional methods in rural settings; and to decrease the isolation of rural teachers and students by giving them greater access to resources and technology.

What this might mean in the long range is using computers to gain access to resources and information that would allow students to broaden their experiences in the humanities. In addition, the involvement of institutions of higher education in the project could lead to greater exposure of the students—many of whom are not oriented toward post-secondary studies—to the possibility of attending college.

In the implementation stage of the project, teams of teachers from 12 rural school districts were matched with college and university faculty members to devise programs. District teams were linked together and to institutions of higher education and other support organizations and to existing networks. Many more school districts applied to participate than could be accommodated; the criteria for selection included strength of leadership by the administration and enthusiasm for the program by teachers.

During the summer of 1987, scholars were chosen to advise the school district team, and the teams began learning how to use computers so that they could have access to the network that was to be created. The South Carolina proposal said specifically that "empowerment" of teachers was a goal so that they would have the authority and ability to shape teaching projects in ways that better met the needs of their students. It was hoped that ultimately students would be exposed to such activities as rural oral history projects, traditional readings in literary and historical texts, and projects placing local legend and myth in new contexts. The aim was to increase not only the sense of community and cultural awareness of students, but also their chances to pursue higher education.

For further information about the program, readers may contact: South Carolina Committee for the Humanities, 6 Monckton Boulevard, P.O. Box 6925, Columbia, SC 29260 (803-738-1850).

REFERENCES

A Foundation Goes to School: The Ford Foundation Comprehensive School Improvement Program. New York: Ford Foundation, 1972.

A Nation at Risk: The Imperative for Educational Reform. A Report to the Nation and the Secretary of Education by the National Commission on Excellence in Education. Washington, D.C.: U.S. Department of Education, 1983, pp. 24–31.

Anrig, Gregory. "Teachers Need Recognition, Support, Autonomy in the Classroom." Interview in *Education Daily.* Jan. 23, 1987, p. 6.

Association for Supervision and Curriculum Development. *Curriculum Update.* Alexandria, Va.: ASCD, 1986.

Barnett, Bruce. "Subordinate Teacher Power in School Organizations." *Sociology of Education.* Vol. 57, No. 1, 1984, pp. 43–55.

Berman, Paul and McLaughlin, Milbrey Wallin. *Federal Programs Supporting Educational Change, Vol. VIII: Implementing and Sustaining Innovations.* Washington, D.C.: U.S. Department of Health, Education and Welfare, May 1978.

Berry, Barnett. "Why Bright College Students Won't Teach." *The Urban Review.* Vol. 18, No. 4, 1986, pp. 269–80.

Boyer, Ernest L. *High School: A Report on Secondary Education in America.* New York: Harper & Row, 1983, p. 159.

Burbules, Nicholas C. "A Theory of Power in Education." *Educational Theory.* Vol. 36, Spring 1986, pp. 95–114.

Carnegie Forum on Education and the Economy. *A Nation Prepared: Teachers for the 21st Century.* The Report of the Task Force on Teaching as a Profession. New York: Carnegie Corporation, 1986.

Chall, Jeanne S. "The Teacher as Scholar." *The Reading Teacher.* Vol. 39, April 1986, pp. 792–97.

Christie, Samuel G. "Beyond Teacher Militancy: Implications for Change Within the School," in *The Power to Change: Issues for the Innovative Educator.* Carmen M. Culver and Gary J. Hoban, eds. New York: McGraw-Hill Book Company, 1973, pp. 140–41.

Chronicle of Higher Education. "Alliances Are Formed in Several Fields." Jan. 7, 1987, p. 13.

Clark, Burton. "The High School and the University: What Went Wrong in America, Part 1." *Phi Delta Kappan.* Feb. 1985, pp. 393–94.

Common, Dianne L. "Power: The Missing Concept in the Dominant Model of School Change." *Theory Into Practice.* Vol. 22, No. 3, 1983, pp. 203–10.

Cummins, Jim. "Empowering Minority Students: A Framework for Intervention." *Harvard Educational Review.* Vol. 56, No. 1, 1986, pp. 18–35.

Daresh, John C. "Staff Development — Guidelines for the Principal." *NASSP Bulletin.* March 1987, p. 22.

DuFour, Richard P. "Must Principals Choose Between Teacher Morale and an Effective School?" *NASSP Bulletin.* May 1986, p. 35.

Education Commission of the States. *What Next? More Leverage for Teachers.* Joslyn Green, ed. Denver: Education Commission of the States, 1986, p. 22.

Elsberg, Ted. "New York 'Master Teacher' Plan Is Self-Defeating." Letter to the Editor in *New York Times.* Dec. 24, 1986.

Fantini, Mario D. *Regaining Excellence in Education.* Columbus: Merrill Publishing Company, 1986, p. 205.

Fullan, Michael. *The Meaning of Educational Change.* New York: Teachers College Press, 1982.

Futrell, Mary H. "NEA President Futrell Stresses Equity in Recruiting and Retaining Teachers." News release by National Education Association. Washington, D.C., Mar. 16, 1987.

Gaudiani, Claire L. and Burnett, David G. *Academic Alliances: A New Approach to School/College Collaboration.* Washington, D.C.: American Association for Higher Education, 1986, p. 5.

Gold, Gerald G. "A Reform Strategy for Education: Employer-Sponsored Teacher Internships." *Phi Delta Kappan.* Jan. 1987, pp. 384–87.

Goodlad, John I. *A Place Called School: Prospects for the Future.* New York: McGraw-Hill Book Company, 1984, p. 168.

Gough, Pauline B. "The Key to Improving Schools: An Interview with William Glasser." *Phi Delta Kappan.* May 1987, pp. 657–58.

Hawley, Willis D. "Horses Before Carts: Developing Adaptive Schools and the Limits of Innovation," in *Making Change Happen?* Dale Mann, ed. New York: Teachers College Press, 1978, p. 236.

Hechinger, Fred M. "Better Schools: Issues of Power." *New York Times.* Sept. 23, 1986, p. C9.

Henson, Kenneth T. "Strategies for Overcoming Barriers to Educational Change." *NASSP Bulletin.* March 1987, pp. 125–27.

Hersey, Paul; Blanchard, Kenneth; and Natemayer, Walter. *Situational Leadership, Perception and the Impact of Power.* La Jolla, Calif.: Center for Leadership Studies, 1979.

Herzberg, Frederick. "How Do You Motivate Employees?" *Harvard Business Review.* Jan.–Feb. 1968, pp. 53–62.

Herzberg, Frederick. *Work and the Nature of Man.* New York: World Publishing Company, 1966.

Hoffman, Ellen. *Teachers and Community Service: A Plus for Both*. Washington, D.C.: Education Writers Association, 1987.

Holmes Group Report. *Tomorrow's Teachers*. East Lansing, Mich.: The Holmes Group, 1986.

Johnson, Susan Moore and Nelson, Niall C. W. "Teaching Reform in an Active Voice." *Phi Delta Kappan*. April 1987, pp. 591–98.

Jwaideh, Alice R. "The Principal as a Facilitator of Change." *Educational Horizons*. Fall 1984, pp. 9–15.

Karp, Jonathan. "Rally Cheers On Fairfax Teachers." *Washington Post*. Aug. 26, 1986, p. B1.

Kerchner, Charles T. and Mitchell, Douglas E. "Teaching Reform and Union Reform." *The Elementary School Journal*. Mar. 1986, pp. 449–70.

Lezotte, Lawrence. "Effective Schools — What Works and Doesn't Work." *New York Teacher*. Mar. 16, 1987, pp. 4–5.

Lieberman, Ann. "Collaborative Work: Working With, Not Working On. . . . " *Educational Leadership*. Feb. 1986, pp. 4–8.

Lightfoot, Sara Lawrence. *The Good High School: Portraits of Character and Culture*. New York: Basic Books, 1983.

Little, Judith Warren. "Norms of Collegiality and Experimentation: Workplace Conditions of School Success." *American Educational Research Journal*. Fall 1982, pp. 325–40.

McDonald, Joseph P. "Raising the Teacher's Voice and the Ironic Role of Theory." *Harvard Educational Review*. Vol. 56, No. 4, 1986, p. 356.

McLaughlin, Milbrey Wallin. "Implementation as Mutual Adaptation: Change in Classroom Organization," in *Making Change Happen?* Dale Mann, ed. New York: Teachers College Press, 1978, pp. 19–31.

McNeil, Linda M. *Contradictions of Control: School Structure and School Knowledge*. New York: Routledge & Keegan Paul, 1986, pp. 157–90.

McMillen, Liz. "Alliances of Teachers and Faculty Members Create Links Between Schools and Colleges." *Chronicle of Higher Education*. Jan. 7, 1987, p. 11.

Maeroff, Gene I. *Don't Blame the Kids: The Trouble with America's Public Schools*. New York: McGraw-Hill Book Company, 1982.

Maeroff, Gene I. *School and College: Partnerships in Education*. Princeton, N.J.: The Carnegie Foundation for the Advancement of Teaching, 1983.

Marburger, Carl L. *One School at a Time: School Based Management — A Process for Change*. Columbia, Md.: National Commission for Citizens in Education, 1985, p. 20.

Marquand, Robert. "Speaking for Teacher Professionalism." *Christian Science Monitor*. Oct. 6, 1986, p. 27.

Metropolitan Life Survey of the American Teacher 1986. Conducted by Louis Harris and Associates, Inc. New York: Metropolitan Life, 1986, p. 42.

Miles, Matthew B. and Lake, D. G. "Self-Renewal in School Systems: A Strategy for Planned Change," in *Concepts for Social Change*. Goodwin B. Watson, ed. Washington, D.C.: COPED by NTL, NEA, 1967, p. 82.

Muth, Rodney. "Toward an Integrative Theory of Power and Educational Organization." *Educational Administration Quarterly*. Spring 1984, pp. 25–42.

National Commission on Excellence in Educational Administration. *Leaders for America's Schools*. Tempe, Ariz.: The University Council for Educational Administration, 1987.

National Executive Service Corps Study. *Education Daily*. Mar. 26, 1987, p. 1.

Pauly, Edward W. "The Decision to Innovate: Career Pursuit as an Incentive for Educational Change," in *Making Change Happen?* Dale Mann, ed. New York: Teachers College Press, 1978, p. 264.

Powell, Arthur G. et al. *The Shopping Mall High School*. Boston: Houghton Mifflin Company, 1985, pp. 70–76.

Presseisen, Barbara Z. *Unlearned Lessons: Current and Past Reforms for School Improvement*. Philadelphia: The Falmer Press, 1985, p. 115.

Public Education Fund. *Second Interim Evaluation Report*. Prepared by Kent McGuire, Milbrey McLaughlin, and Paul Nechtigal (team leader). 1986, pp. 15–16.

Romberg, Thomas A. and Pitman, Allan. *Annual Report to the Ford Foundation: The Urban Mathematics Collaborative Projects*. Madison, Wisc.: University of Wisconsin, 1985; p. 15.

Romberg, Thomas A. et al. *1986 Annual Report to the Ford Foundation: The Urban Mathematics Collaborative Project*. Madison, Wisc.: University of Wisconsin, 1987.

Sarason, Seymour B. *The Culture of the School and the Problem of Change*. 2d Ed. Boston: Allyn and Bacon, 1982.

Sava, Samuel. "Leader of School Principals Calls Carnegie Report Naive." *Education Daily*. July 28, 1986, p. 2.

Shanker, Albert. "Real Teachers Need Real Training." Advertisement in *New York Times*. Aug. 10, 1986, sec. IV, p. 7.

Sizer, Theodore R. *Horace's Compromise: The Dilemma of the American High School*. Boston: Houghton Mifflin Company, 1984, p. 183.

Smith, Frank. *Insult to Intelligence*. New York: Arbor House, 1986, pp. x, 12, and 126.

Soler, Carole Hannah. "You Can't Argue Epistemology With the Board of Education." Letter to the Editor in *New York Times*. Mar. 16, 1987.

Teacher Development in Schools: A Report to the Ford Foundation. New York: Academy for Educational Development, 1985, p. 8.

Tozer, Steve. "Dominant Ideology and the Teacher's Authority." *Contemporary Education*. Spring 1985, pp. 148–53.

Ventures in Good Schooling: A Cooperative Model for a Successful Secondary School. Reston, Va.: National Association of Secondary School Principals and National Education Association, 1986.

Woodring, Paul. "Too Bright to Be a Teacher?" *Phi Delta Kappan*. April 1987, p. 617.

Woodrow Wilson National Fellowship Foundation. *Teachers Teaching Teachers*. Princeton, N.J.: WWNFF, 1986.

Woodside, William S. "William S. Woodside on the Corporate Role." Interview in *New York Times*. July 13, 1986, sec. IV, p. 8.

INDEX

ABOUT THE AUTHOR

GENE I. MAEROFF was education writer of *The New York Times* from 1971 through 1986. He is now senior fellow at the Carnegie Foundation for the Advancement of Teaching in Princeton, New Jersey. His previous books are *School and College, Don't Blame the Kids*, and the *Guide to Suburban Public Schools*. His articles have appeared in many magazines of both general and educational interest. Among them are *The New York Times Magazine, Town & Country, Seventeen, Saturday Review, The Nation, Parade, New York Magazine, Working Mother, Parents, Ladies' Home Journal, Phi Delta Kappan, The Reading Teacher, Change, Education Week, Educational Record, Education Digest*, and *Secondary School Principals Bulletin*. Included among the awards that Maeroff has won are those from the Education Writers Association, the International Reading Association, and the American Association of University Professors. He is a member of the advisory boards to ERIC and to the Institute for Educational Management at Harvard University, as well as a long-time member of the Higher Education Seminar of Columbia University. Maeroff resides in Manhattan and is the father of two daughters, Janine and Rachel, and a son, Adam.